Collins

Teacher's Guide 6
Comprehension Skills

Author: Abigail Steel

William Collins' dream of knowledge for all began with the publication of his first book in 1819.

A self-educated mill worker, he not only enriched millions of lives, but also founded a flourishing publishing house. Today, staying true to this spirit, Collins books are packed with inspiration, innovation and practical expertise. They place you at the centre of a world of possibility and give you exactly what you need to explore it.

Collins. Freedom to teach.

An imprint of HarperCollins*Publishers*
The News Building
1 London Bridge Street
London
SE1 9GF

Browse the complete Collins catalogue at
www.collins.co.uk

© HarperCollins*Publishers* Limited 2017

10 9 8 7 6 5 4 3 2 1

ISBN 978-0-00-822295-6

All rights reserved. No part of this publication may be reproduced, stored in a retrieval system, or transmitted in any form or by any means, electronic, mechanical, photocopying, recording or otherwise, without the prior written permission of the Publisher or a licence permitting restricted copying in the United Kingdom issued by the Copyright Licensing Agency Ltd., 90 Tottenham Court Road, London W1T 4LP.

British Library Cataloguing in Publication Data

A catalogue record for this publication is available from the British Library.

Publisher: Lee Newman
Publishing Manager: Helen Doran
Senior Editor: Hannah Dove
Project Manager: Emily Hooton
Author: Abigail Steel
Development Editor: Hannah Hirst-Dunton
Copy-editor: Tanya Solomons
Proofreader: Ros and Chris Davies
Illustrations: Aptara, Beatriz Castro and QBS
Cover design and artwork: Amparo Barrera and Ken Vail Graphic Design
Illustrations: Aptara, Beatriz Castro and QBS
Internal design concept: Amparo Barrera
Typesetter: 2Hoots Publishing Services Ltd
Production Controller: Rachel Weaver

Printed and bound by CPI Group (UK) Ltd, Croydon, CR0 4YY

Acknowledgements

The publishers wish to thank the following for permission to reproduce content. Every effort has been made to trace copyright holders and to obtain their permission for the use of copyright materials. The publishers will gladly receive any information enabling them to rectify any error or omission at the first opportunity.

David Higham Associates Ltd for extracts on pages 22–24 from *Trouble Half-Way* by Jan Mark, Penguin Books, 1985. Reproduced by permission of David Higham Associates Ltd; Mrs A. W. Morse for the poem on pages 34–36 from "Crack-a-dawn" by Brian Morse, published in *Picnic on the Moon*, Turton and Chambers Ltd, 1990. Granted by kind permission of Mrs A. W. Morse; The Society of Authors for the poem on pages 40–42 "The Highwayman" by Alfred Noyes. Reproduced by The Society of Authors as the Literary Representation of the Estate of Alfred Noyes; HarperCollins Publishers Ltd for the extract on page 43 from *Selim-Hassan the Seventh and The Wall* by Vivian French, copyright © 2008 Vivian French. Reproduced by permission of HarperCollins Publishers Ltd.; Carlton Books Ltd and Curtis Brown Group, Inc for the poem on pages 51–53 and 106 "Winter Morning" by Ogden Nash from *Candy is Dandy, The Best of Ogden Nash*, Carlton Books Ltd, 1994 and Parents Keep Out, 2nd edition, Little Brown and Co, 1951, copyright © 1962 by Ogden Nash, renewed. Reproduced by permission of Carlton Books Ltd and Curtis Brown, Ltd; HarperCollins Publishers Ltd and Penguin Random House for extracts on pages 54–56 from *The Phantom Tollbooth* by Norton Juster, text copyright © 1961, © renewed 1989 by Norton Juster. Reproduced by permission of HarperCollins Publishers Ltd and Random House Children's Books, a division of Penguin Random House LLC. All rights reserved; HarperCollins Publishers Ltd for the extract on page 66 from *Swimming the Dream* by Ellie Simmonds, copyright © 2012 HarperCollins. Reproduced by permission of HarperCollins Publishers Ltd; HarperCollins Publishers Ltd and Aitken Alexander Associates Ltd for extracts on pages 68–70 from *Wild Swans: Three Daughters of China* by Jung Chang, published by HarperCollins, copyright © Jung Chang and Globalflair Ltd. Reproduced by permission of HarperCollins Publishers Ltd and Aitken Alexander Associates Ltd; and Peters Fraser & Dunlop for the poem on pages 71–73 and 118 'Rebecca, Who Slammed Doors for Fun and Perished Miserably' from *Cautionary Tales for Children* by Hilaire Belloc. Reprinted by permission of Peters Fraser & Dunlop (www.petersfraserdunlop.com) on behalf of the Estate of Hilaire Belloc. HarperCollins Publishers Ltd for the extract on page 75 from *Project Bright Spark* by Annabel Pitcher, copyright © 2013 Annabel Pitcher; the extract on page 78 from *The 39 Steps* by Andrew Lane, copyright © 2016 Andrew Lane; the extract on pages 80–81 from *Benjamin Zephaniah: My Story* by Benjamin Zephaniah, copyright © 2011 Benjamin Zephaniah; the extract on page 84 from *The Kingdom of Benin* by Philip Steele, copyright © 2015 Philip Steele; the extracts on page 86 from 'Sullen Jane' and 'Competition' published in *Gathering in the Days* by Gareth Owen, copyright © 2011 Gareth Owen. Reproduced by permission of HarperCollins Publishers Ltd.

Contents

About Treasure House 4

Support, embed and challenge 12

Assessment 13

Support with teaching comprehension 14

Delivering the 2014 National Curriculum for English 16

Unit 1: Fiction: 'Trouble Half-Way' 22

Unit 2: Fiction (traditional): 'The Discontented Fish' 25

Unit 3: Non-fiction (persuasive writing): Advertisements 28

Unit 4: Non-fiction (emails): Climate change, what climate change? 31

Unit 5: Poetry: 'Crack-a-Dawn' 34

Unit 6: Poetry: 'The Song of Hiawatha' 37

Unit 7: Poetry: 'The Highwayman' 40

Review unit 1: Fiction: 'Selim-Hassan the Seventh' 43

Unit 8: Non-fiction (news report): Save it! 45

Unit 9: Non-fiction (information text): Deserts 48

Unit 10: Poetry: Views of winter 51

Unit 11: Fiction: 'The Phantom Tollbooth' 54

Unit 12: Fiction (classic): 'The Railway Children' 57

Unit 13: Fiction (classic): 'Gulliver's Travels' 60

Unit 14: Playscript: 'Compere Lapin and Compere Tig' 63

Review unit 2: Non-fiction (autobiography): 'Swimming the Dream' 66

Unit 15: Non-fiction (autobiography): 'Wild Swans' 68

Unit 16: Poetry: 'Rebecca (Who Slammed Doors for Fun and Perished Miserably)' . . . 71

Unit 17: Fiction (modern): 'Project Bright Spark' 74

Unit 18: Fiction: 'The 39 Steps' 77

Unit 19: Non-fiction (autobiography): 'Benjamin Zephaniah: My Story' 80

Unit 20: Non-fiction (information text): 'The Kingdom of Benin' 83

Review unit 3: Poetry: 'Sullen Jane' and 'Competition' 86

Photocopiable resources 88

About Treasure House

Treasure House is a comprehensive and flexible bank of books and online resources for teaching the English curriculum. The Treasure House series offers two different pathways: one covering each English strand discretely (Skills Focus Pathway) and one integrating texts and the strands to create a programme of study (Integrated English Pathway). This Teacher's Guide is part of the Skills Focus Pathway.

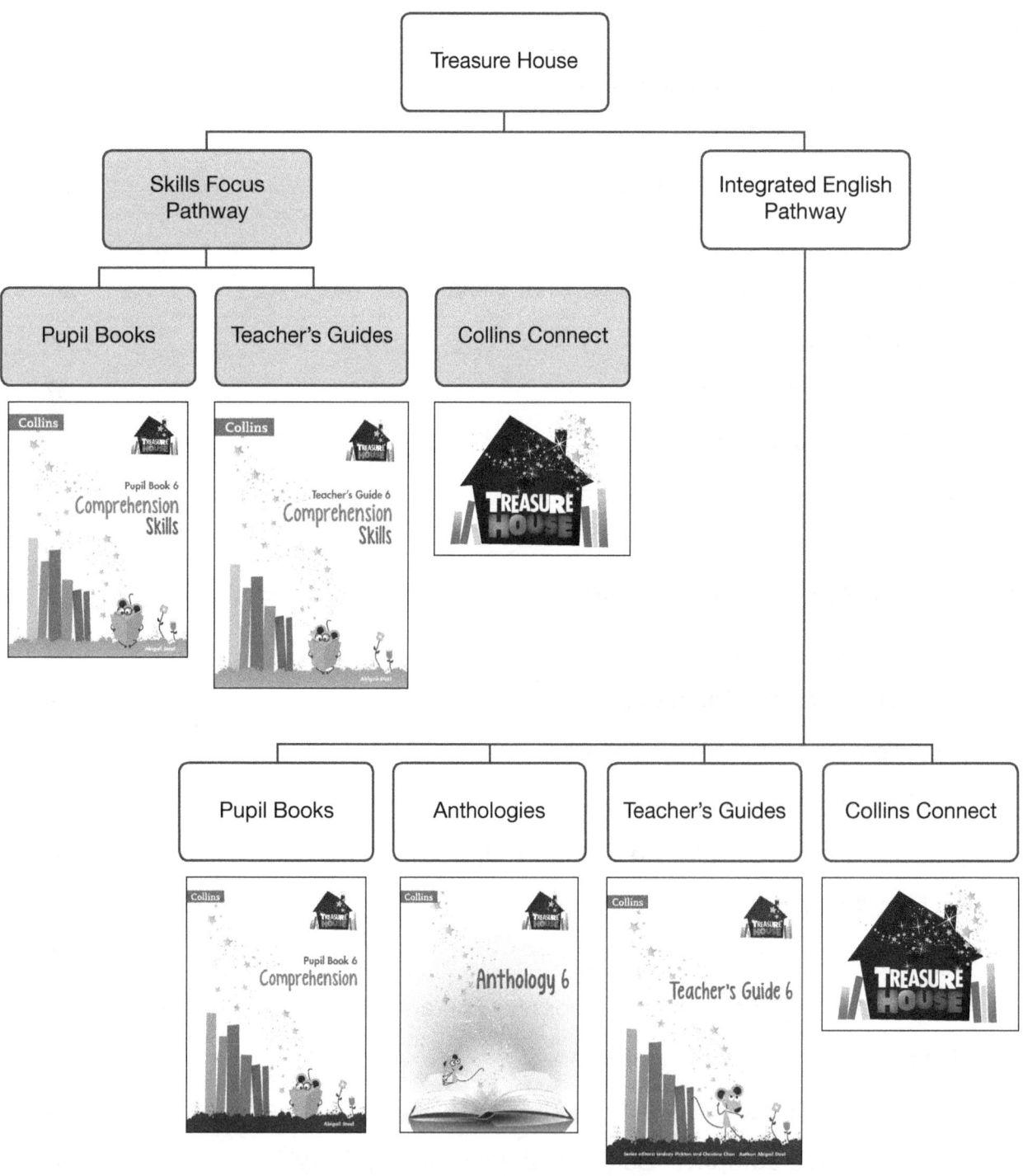

About Treasure House

1. Skills Focus

The Skills Focus Pupil Books and Teacher's Guides for all four strands (Comprehension; Spelling; Composition; and Vocabulary, Grammar and Punctuation) allow you to teach each curriculum area in a targeted way. Each unit in the Pupil Book is mapped directly to the statutory requirements of the National Curriculum. Each Teacher's Guide provides step-by-step instructions to guide you through the Pupil Book activities and digital Collins Connect resources for each competency. With a clear focus on skills and clearly-listed curriculum objectives you can select the appropriate resources to support your lessons.

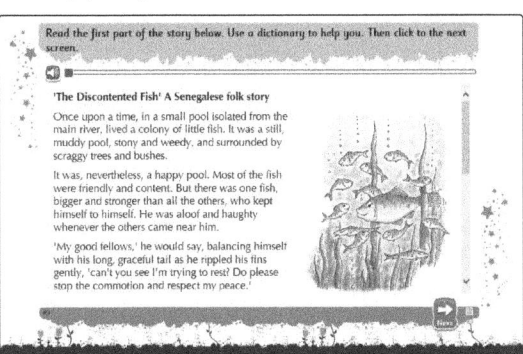

2. Integrated English

Alternatively, the Integrated English pathway offers a complete programme of genre-based teaching sequences. There is one Teacher's Guide and one Anthology for each year group. Each Teacher's Guide provides 15 teaching sequences focused on different genres of text such as fairy tales, letters and newspaper articles. The Anthologies contain the classic texts, fiction, non-fiction and poetry required for each sequence. Each sequence also weaves together all four dimensions of the National Curriculum for English – Comprehension; Spelling; Composition; and Vocabulary, Grammar and Punctuation – into a complete English programme. The Pupil Books and Collins Connect provide targeted explanation of key points and practice activities organised by strand. This programme provides 30 weeks of teaching inspiration.

Other components

Handwriting Books, Handwriting Workbooks and the online digital resources on Collins Connect are suitable for use with both pathways.

About Treasure House

Treasure House Skills Focus Teacher's Guides

Year	Comprehension	Composition	Vocabulary, Grammar and Punctuation	Spelling
1	978-0-00-822290-1	978-0-00-822302-1	978-0-00-822296-3	978-0-00-822308-3
2	978-0-00-822291-8	978-0-00-822303-8	978-0-00-822297-0	978-0-00-822309-0
3	978-0-00-822292-5	978-0-00-822304-5	978-0-00-822298-7	978-0-00-822310-6
4	978-0-00-822293-2	978-0-00-822305-2	978-0-00-822299-4	978-0-00-822311-3
5	978-0-00-822294-9	978-0-00-822306-9	978-0-00-822300-7	978-0-00-822312-0
6	978-0-00-822295-6	978-0-00-822307-6	978-0-00-822301-4	978-0-00-822313-7

About Treasure House

Inside the Skills Focus Teacher's Guides

The teaching notes in each unit of the Teacher's Guide provide you with subject information or background, a range of whole class and differentiated activities including photocopiable resource sheets and links to the Pupil Book and the online Collins Connect activities.

Each **Overview** provides clear objectives for each lesson tied into the new curriculum, links to the other relevant components and a list of any additional resources required.

Pupil practice gives guidance and the answers to each of the three sections in the Pupil Book: *Get started*, *Try these* and *Now try these*.

Support, embed & challenge supports a mastery approach with activities provided at three levels.

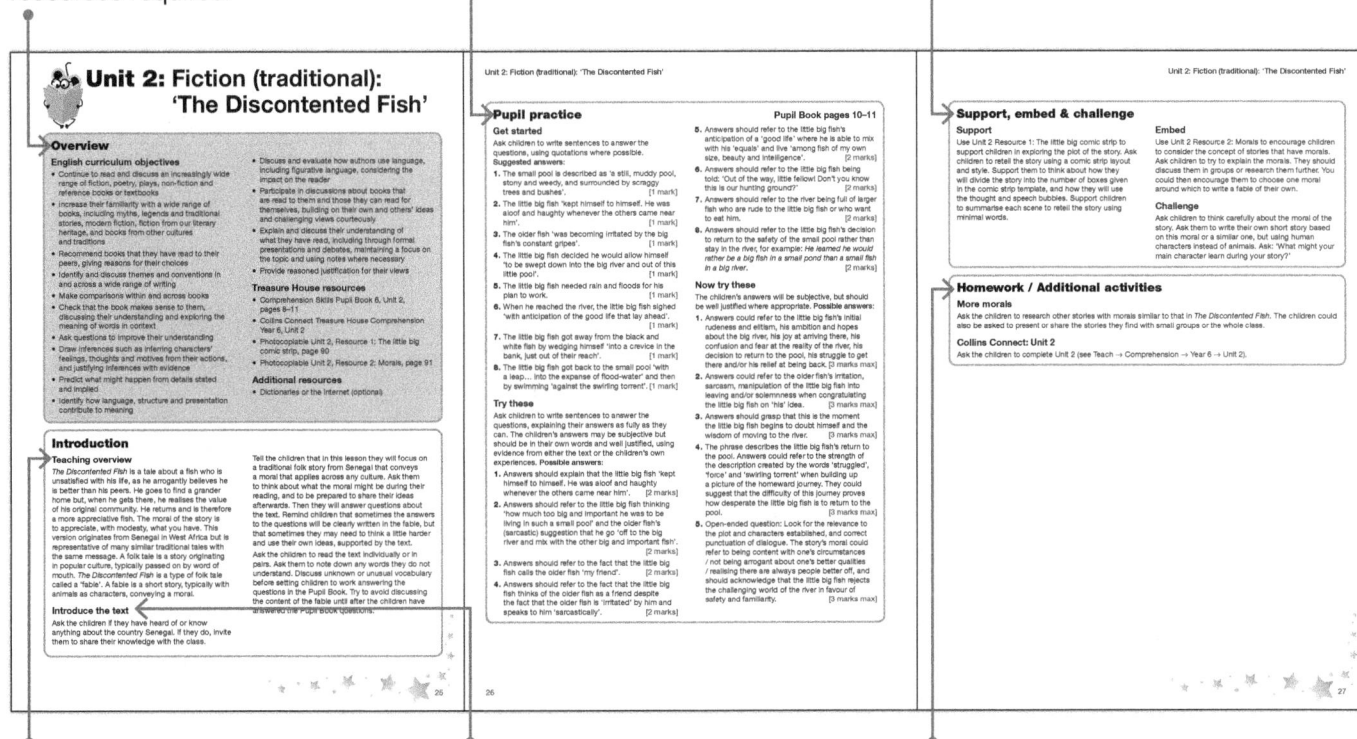

Teaching overview provides a brief introduction to the specific skill concept or text type and some pointers on how to approach it.

Introduce the concept/text provides 5–10 minutes of preliminary discussion points or class/group activities to get the pupils engaged in the lesson focus and set out any essential prior learning.

Homework / Additional activities lists ideas for classroom or homework activities, and relevant activities from Collins Connect.

Two photocopiable **resource** worksheets per unit provide extra practice of the specific lesson concept. They are designed to be used with the activities in support, embed or challenge sections.

About Treasure House

Treasure House Skills Focus Pupil Books

There are four Skills Focus Pupil Books for each year group, based on the four dimensions of the National Curriculum for English: Comprehension; Spelling; Composition; and Vocabulary, Grammar and Punctuation. The Pupil Books provide a child-friendly introduction to each subject and a range of initial activities for independent pupil-led learning. A Review unit for each term assesses pupils' progress.

Year	Comprehension	Composition	Vocabulary, Grammar and Punctuation	Spelling
1	978-0-00-823634-2	978-0-00-823646-5	978-0-00-823640-3	978-0-00-823652-6
2	978-0-00-823635-9	978-0-00-823647-2	978-0-00-823641-0	978-0-00-823653-3
3	978-0-00-823636-6	978-0-00-823648-9	978-0-00-823642-7	978-0-00-823654-0
4	978-0-00-823637-3	978-0-00-823649-6	978-0-00-823643-4	978-0-00-823655-7
5	978-0-00-823638-0	978-0-00-823650-2	978-0-00-823644-1	978-0-00-823656-4
6	978-0-00-823639-7	978-0-00-823651-9	978-0-00-823645-8	978-0-00-823657-1

About Treasure House

Inside the Skills Focus Pupil Books

Comprehension

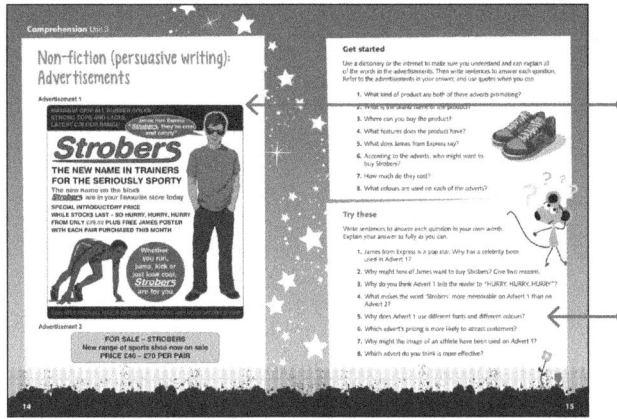

Includes high-quality text extracts covering poetry, prose, traditional tales, playscripts and non-fiction.

Pupils retrieve and record information, learn to draw inferences from texts and increase their familiarity with a wide range of literary genres.

Composition

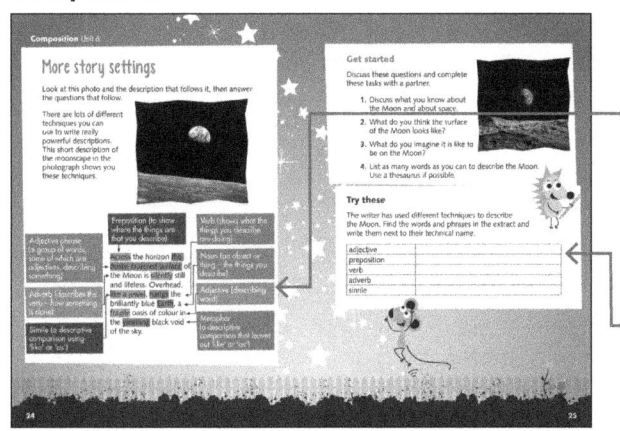

Includes high-quality, annotated text extracts as models for different types of writing.

Children learn how to write effectively and for a purpose.

Vocabulary, Grammar and Punctuation

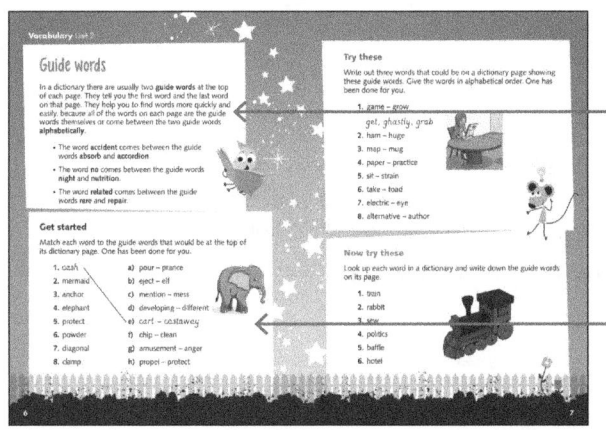

Develops children's knowledge and understanding of grammar and punctuation skills.

A rule is introduced and explained. Children are given lots of opportunities to practise using it.

Spelling

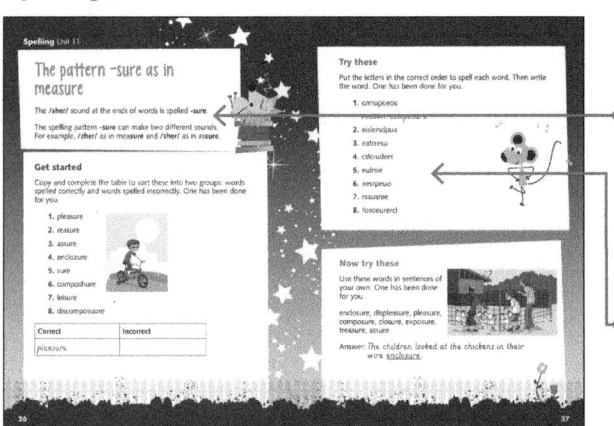

Spelling rules are introduced and explained.

Practice is provided for spotting and using the spelling rules, correcting misspelt words and using the words in context.

About Treasure House

Treasure House on Collins Connect

Digital resources for Treasure House are available on Collins Connect which provides a wealth of interactive activities. Treasure House is organised into six core areas on Collins Connect:

- Comprehension
- Spelling
- Composition
- Vocabulary, Grammar and Punctuation
- The Reading Attic
- Teacher's Guides and Anthologies.

For most units in the Skills Focus Pupil Books, there is an accompanying Collins Connect unit focused on the same teaching objective. These fun, independent activities can be used for initial pupil-led learning, or for further practice using a different learning environment. Either way, with Collins Connect, you have a wealth of questions to help children embed their learning.

Treasure House on Collins Connect is available via subscription at connect.collins.co.uk

Features of Treasure House on Collins Connect

The digital resources enhance children's comprehension, spelling, composition, and vocabulary, grammar, punctuation skills through providing:

- a bank of varied and engaging interactive activities so children can practise their skills independently
- audio support to help children access the texts and activities
- auto-mark functionality so children receive instant feedback and have the opportunity to repeat tasks.

Teachers benefit from useful resources and time-saving tools including:

- teacher-facing materials such as audio and explanations for front-of-class teaching or pupil-led learning
- lesson starter videos for some Composition units
- downloadable teaching notes for all online activities
- downloadable teaching notes for Skills Focus and Integrated English pathways
- the option to assign homework activities to your classes
- class records to monitor progress.

Comprehension

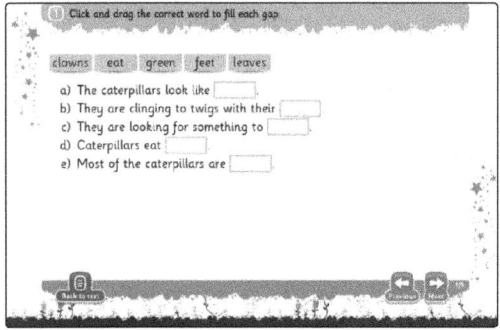

- Includes high-quality text extracts covering poetry, prose, traditional tales, playscripts and non-fiction.
- Audio function supports children to access the text and the activities

Composition

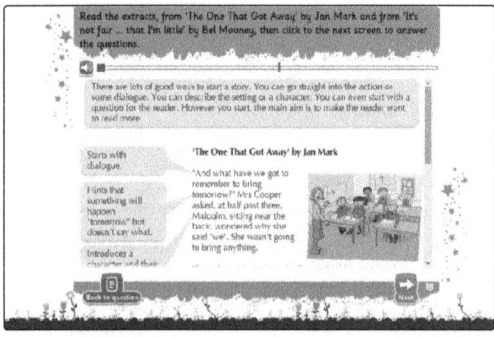

- Activities support children to develop and build more sophisticated sentence structures.
- Every unit ends with a longer piece of writing that can be submitted to the teacher for marking.

About Treasure House

Vocabulary, Grammar and Punctuation

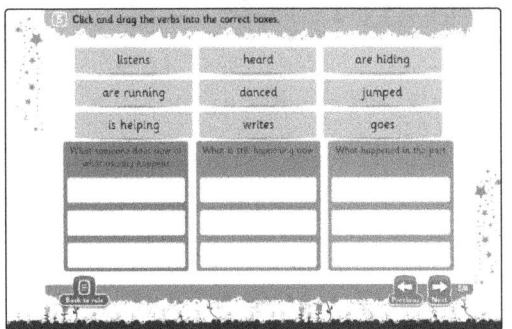

- Fun, practical activities develop children's knowledge and understanding of grammar and punctuation skills.
- Each skill is reinforced with a huge, varied bank of practice questions.

Spelling

- Fun, practical activities develop children's knowledge and understanding of each spelling rule.
- Each rule is reinforced with a huge, varied bank of practice questions.
- Children spell words using an audio prompt, write their own sentences and practise spelling using Look Say Cover Write Check.

Reading Attic

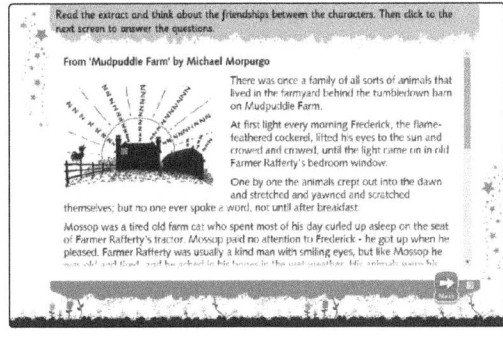

- Children's love of reading is nurtured with texts from exciting children's authors including Micheal Bond, David Walliams and Micheal Morpurgo.
- Lesson sequences accompany the texts, with drama opportunities and creative strategies for engaging children with key themes, characters and plots.
- Whole-book projects encourage reading for pleasure.

Treasure House Digital Teacher's Guides and Anthologies

The teaching sequences and anthology texts for each year group are included as a flexible bank of resources.

The teaching notes for each skill strand and year group are also included on Collins Connect.

Support, embed and challenge

Treasure House provides comprehensive, detailed differentiation at three levels to ensure that all children are able to access achievement. It is important that children master the basic skills before they go further in their learning. Children may make progress towards the standard at different speeds, with some not reaching it until the very end of the year.

In the Teacher's Guide, Support, Embed and Challenge sections allow teachers to keep the whole class focussed with no child left behind. Two photocopiable resources per unit offer additional material linked to the Support, Embed or Challenge sections.

Support

The Support section offers simpler or more scaffolded activities that will help learners who have not yet grasped specific concepts covered. Background information may also be provided to help children to contextualise learning. This enables children to make progress so that they can keep up with the class.

To help with reading comprehension, some support activities help learners to access the core text, for example, by giving some background information to the story or support with figurative speech. This is more motivating and enjoyable than offering a simplified text.

If you have a teaching assistant, you may wish to ask him or her to help children work through these activities. You might then ask children who have completed these activities to progress to other more challenging tasks found in the Embed or Challenge sections – or you may decide more practice of the basics is required. Collins Connect can provide further activities.

Embed

The Embed section includes activities to embed learning and is aimed at those who children who are working at the expected standard. It ensures that learners have understood key teaching objectives for the age-group. These activities could be used by the whole class or groups, and most are appropriate for both teacher-led and independent work.

In Comprehension, all children should cross the threshold of reading the texts in Treasure House; however, the depth of their analysis and understanding will vary depending on prior experience, current interests and motivation. Activities in the Embed section encourage children to apply their learning by further analysing the text or by planning their own writing based on the same theme or text-type.

Challenge

The Challenge section provides additional tasks, questions or activities that will push children who have mastered the concept without difficulty. This keeps children motivated and allows them to gain a greater depth of understanding. You may wish to give these activities to fast finishers to work through independently.

In Comprehension, children explore the text-type or theme further through drama, research, discussion or by doing their own writing.

Assessment

Teacher's Guide

There are opportunities for assessment throughout the Treasure House series. The teaching notes in Treasure House Teacher's Guides offer ideas for questions, informal assessment and spelling tests.

Pupil Book Review units

Each Pupil Book has three Review units designed as a quick formative assessment tool for the end of each term. Questions assess the work that has been covered over the previous units. These review units will provide you with an informal way of measuring your pupils' progress. You may wish to use these as Assessment for Learning to help you and your pupils to understand where they are in their learning journey.

The Review units in the Comprehension Pupil Books provide children with a new text or extract to read and understand. Children can draw on what they have learned during the term to help them access the new text without an initial teaching session to guide them. Questions types may reoccur across the Review units allowing you to see progression across the year, and the three reviews will always cover all three genres: fiction, non-fiction and poetry.

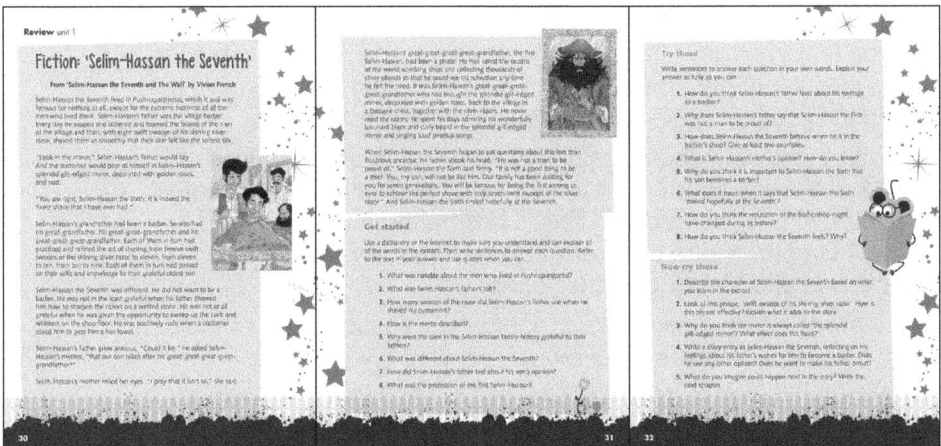

Assessment in Collins Connect

Activities on Collins Connect can also be used for effective assessment. Activities with auto-marking mean that if children answer incorrectly, they can make another attempt helping them to analyse their own work for mistakes. Homework activities can also be assigned to classes through Collins Connect. At the end of activities, children can select a smiley face to indicate how they found the task giving you useful feedback on any gaps in knowledge.

Class records on Collins Connect allow you to get an overview of children's progress with several features. You can choose to view records by unit, pupil or strand. By viewing detailed scores, you can view pupils' scores question by question in a clear table-format to help you establish areas where there might be particular strengths and weaknesses both class-wide and for individuals.

If you wish, you can also set mastery judgements (mastery achieved and exceeded, mastery achieved, mastery not yet achieved) to help see where your children need more help.

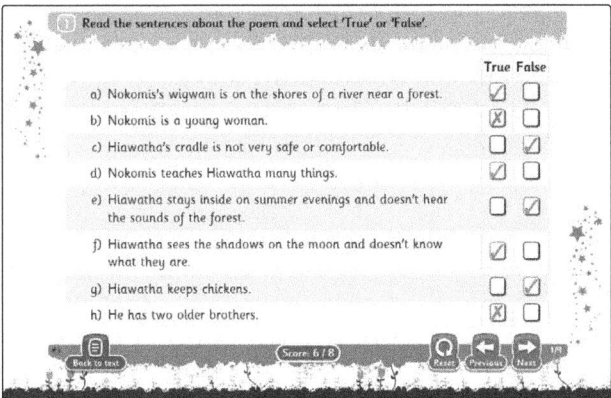

Support with teaching comprehension

The teacher's guides for Comprehension units can be followed in a simple linear fashion that structures the lesson into five sections:

- assessment of existing skills and knowledge, and an introduction to the unit's source text
- reading the source text
- completion of the 'pupil practice' questions
- differentiated work, following the Support, Embed and Challenge activity guidance (using the provided photocopiable worksheets)
- homework or additional activities.

However, this lesson structure is intended to be flexible. While we recommend that the first three of these steps should usually be followed in the given order, work following the pupil practice questions can be manipulated in numerous ways to suit the needs, skills and preferences of your class.

For example, you may wish to set one of the differentiation activities as homework for the whole class, or to guide children through an 'additional' activity during the lesson, rather than setting it as homework. You may alternatively judge that your class has firmly grasped the concept being taught, and choose not to use any activity suggested, or perhaps introduce only the Extend activity: it is not essential that every activity outlined in the teacher's guide units should be completed.

With the same motivation, many activities (and worksheets) could be adapted for reuse in units other than the one for which they are provided. Several activity and worksheet types are already repeated in similar forms between (and sometimes within) year groups. This is in order both to show the children's changing levels of attainment directly, and to allow any children who have found an activity challenging to reattempt it in a new context after developing their skills.

If, however, children find a particular activity either challenging or particularly engaging, you should also feel free to repeat that activity, where appropriate, at your own discretion. For example, if children enjoy considering appropriate costumes and settings when looking at a playscript (an activity, with worksheet, suggested in Year 3 Unit 17), this activity could be adapted to fit any playscript source text – and many prose fiction texts, too.

You may also wish to consider using Support activities in conjunction with the pupil practice questions, if children are struggling with content or a concept with which the Support activity deals. For example, if questions within the 'Try these' and 'Now try these' sections of pupil practice require understanding of similes, you may wish to intervene and prepare children using an appropriate Support activity (such as suggested in Year 3 Unit 2).

By using the teacher's guide units and their suggested activities flexibly, you can choose to tailor the resources at your fingertips to provide the most beneficial learning system for the children being taught.

Teaching comprehension is a key part of achieving the universal aim of developing children's love of literature through widespread reading for enjoyment. If children are confident and fluent readers, who understand the form and content of the texts they read they are more likely to enjoy them.

We can make learning comprehension easy and fun by employing simple techniques to guide children along their reading journey.

Modelling

When reading a letter or newspaper article to the class remember to hesitate on words that they might not know, intimate that you are unsure of the proper meaning and look them up in a dictionary. You might also model how you use context or grammar clues to work out the meaning using the rest of the text.

Making predictions

When embarking on any new text ask children to consider what they think it will be about, or what they think might happen. Show how to look for clues in the presentation of the text or the introductory information you have. Remember to model making your own predictions too – this gives you an opportunity to demonstrate how to rationalize a prediction by speaking your thought processes aloud.

Questioning

Questioning can take many forms and penetrate many depths of understanding. Questions can be closed, requiring short, defined answers or they can be open, enabling the children to explore wider thoughts. Sometimes the best questions are those that are spontaneous and form part of a natural conversation exploring a text. Encourage children to form their own questions about the purpose, structure and content of texts – they could note these down and return to them later to see if they have discovered the answers after reading.

Retelling and summarizing

Encourage children to reflect upon what has happened in a text – this can be a surprisingly challenging activity. Provide plenty of demonstrations of how to retell and summarize. Retelling and summarizing can take many fun, interactive forms such as role play, radio presentations, creating news flash articles, and oral story retellings. Some children struggle with sequencing and ordering so build this in with your retelling activities.

Visualizing

When we read we create mental images of what is happening. Descriptions of people, places and action are acted out in our minds. For children this skill doesn't always come naturally. Ask children to close their eyes and focus on imagining how something looks. Compare written texts to the films and TV shows they are familiar with watching. Point out specific adjectives and adverbs that are actively working within the text to assist the reader. Enable children the opportunity to draw and paint their interpretations of the texts they read.

Connections to children's own experiences

Younger children are often better at pointing at when they recognise a similarity between their own life and something they read in a text. Older children tend to become less inward looking and aren't so forthcoming with the links they make to texts. Encourage them by asking direct questions: *Does anyone else recognise this event? Do you know a character like this? Have you ever been to a similar place? When have you felt that emotion like the character?* Making explicit connections with the text can advance children's understanding of not only the event being described but also the history to the event and the character's emotions. They are able to talk about the 'bigger picture'.

Delivering the 2014 National Curriculum for English

English Programme of Study

Reading – comprehension

	Units																			
	1	2	3	4	5	6	7	8	9	10	11	12	13	14	15	16	17	18	19	20
Maintain positive attitudes to reading and understanding of what they read by:																				
Continuing to read and discuss an increasingly wide range of fiction, poetry, plays, non-fiction and reference books or textbooks	✓	✓	✓	✓	✓	✓	✓	✓	✓	✓	✓	✓	✓	✓	✓	✓	✓		✓	✓
Reading books that are structured in different ways and reading for a range of purposes			✓	✓					✓						✓				✓	✓
Increasing their familiarity with a wide range of books, including myths, legends and traditional stories, modern fiction, fiction from our literary heritage, and books from other cultures and traditions	✓	✓						✓			✓	✓	✓	✓			✓	✓		
Recommending books that they have read to their peers, giving reasons for their choices	✓	✓									✓	✓	✓				✓	✓		
Identifying and discussing themes and conventions in and across a wide range of writing	✓	✓	✓	✓	✓	✓	✓			✓	✓	✓	✓	✓	✓		✓	✓	✓	✓
Making comparisons within and across books	✓	✓																✓		
Learning a wider range of poetry by heart					✓	✓	✓			✓						✓				
Preparing poems and plays to read aloud and to perform, showing understanding through intonation, tone and volume so that the meaning is clear to an audience					✓	✓	✓			✓				✓		✓				

English Programme of Study

Reading – comprehension		Units																			
		1	2	3	4	5	6	7	8	9	10	11	12	13	14	15	16	17	18	19	20
Understand what they read by:	Checking that the book makes sense to them, discussing their understanding and exploring the meaning of words in context	✓	✓	✓	✓	✓	✓	✓	✓	✓	✓	✓	✓	✓	✓	✓	✓	✓	✓	✓	✓
	Asking questions to improve their understanding	✓	✓	✓		✓	✓	✓			✓	✓	✓	✓	✓	✓	✓	✓	✓	✓	✓
	Drawing inferences such as inferring characters' feelings, thoughts and motives from their actions, and justifying inferences with evidence	✓	✓			✓		✓			✓						✓	✓	✓			
	Predicting what might happen from details stated and implied	✓	✓									✓		✓				✓	✓			
	Summarising the main ideas drawn from more than one paragraph, identifying key details that support the main ideas			✓					✓	✓						✓					✓	✓
	Identifying how language, structure and presentation contribute to meaning	✓	✓	✓	✓	✓	✓	✓	✓	✓	✓	✓	✓	✓	✓	✓	✓	✓	✓	✓	✓
Discuss and evaluate how authors use language, including figurative language, considering the impact on the reader		✓	✓			✓	✓	✓										✓	✓			
Distinguish between statements of fact and opinion				✓	✓				✓	✓						✓	✓			✓	✓
Retrieve, record and present information from non-fiction				✓	✓				✓	✓						✓				✓	✓
Participate in discussions about books that are read to them and those they can read for themselves, building on their own and others' ideas and challenging views courteously	✓	✓	✓	✓	✓	✓	✓	✓	✓	✓	✓	✓	✓	✓	✓	✓	✓	✓	✓	✓
Explain and discuss their understanding of what they have read, including through formal presentations and debates, maintaining a focus on the topic and using notes where necessary	✓	✓	✓	✓	✓	✓	✓	✓	✓	✓	✓	✓	✓	✓	✓	✓	✓	✓	✓	✓
Provide reasoned justifications for their views.	✓	✓	✓	✓	✓	✓	✓	✓	✓	✓	✓	✓	✓	✓	✓	✓	✓	✓	✓	✓

Treasure House resources overview

Unit	Title	Treasure House Resources	Collins Connect

1	Fiction: 'Trouble Half-Way'	• Comprehension Skills Pupil Book 6, Unit 1, pages 4–7
		• Comprehension Skills Teacher's Guide 6
		  – Unit 1, pages 22–24
		  – Photocopiable Unit 1, Resource 1: Amy's character, page 88
		  – Photocopiable Unit 1, Resource 2: Richard's view, page 89
			Collins Connect Treasure House Comprehension Year 6, Unit 1

2	Fiction (traditional): 'The Discontented Fish'	• Comprehension Skills Pupil Book 6, Unit 2, pages 8–11
		• Comprehension Skills Teacher's Guide 6
		  – Unit 2, pages 25–27
		  – Photocopiable Unit 2, Resource 1: The little big comic strip, page 90
		  – Photocopiable Unit 2, Resource 2: Morals, page 91
			Collins Connect Treasure House Comprehension Year 6, Unit 2

3	Non-fiction (persuasive writing): Advertisements	• Comprehension Skills Pupil Book 6, Unit 3, pages 12–14
		• Comprehension Skills Teacher's Guide 6
		  – Unit 3, pages 28–30
		  – Photocopiable Unit 3, Resource 1: Bike advert, page 92
		  – Photocopiable Unit 3, Resource 2: Bike questionnaire, page 93
			Collins Connect Treasure House Comprehension Year 6, Unit 3

4	Non-fiction (emails): Climate change, what climate change?	• Comprehension Skills Pupil Book 6, Unit 4, pages 15–18
		• Comprehension Skills Teacher's Guide 6
		  – Unit 4, pages 31–33
		  – Photocopiable Unit 4, Resource 1: For and against, page 94
		  – Photocopiable Unit 4, Resource 2: An email to Pete, page 95
			Collins Connect Treasure House Comprehension Year 6, Unit 4

5	Poetry: 'Crack-a-Dawn'	• Comprehension Skills Pupil Book 6, Unit 5, pages 19–21
		• Comprehension Skills Teacher's Guide 6
		  – Unit 5, pages 34–36
		  – Photocopiable Unit 5, Resource 1: Countdown summary, page 96
		  – Photocopiable Unit 5, Resource 2: My countdown poem, page 97
			Collins Connect Treasure House Comprehension Year 6, Unit 5

6	Poetry: 'The Song of Hiawatha'	• Comprehension Skills Pupil Book 6, Unit 6, pages 22–25
		• Comprehension Skills Teacher's Guide 6
		  – Unit 6, pages 37–39
		  – Photocopiable Unit 6, Resource 1: Finding the beat, page 98
		  – Photocopiable Unit 6, Resource 2: Hiawatha's brothers, page 99
			Collins Connect Treasure House Comprehension Year 6, Unit 6

Unit	Title	Treasure House Resources	Collins Connect
7	Poetry: 'The Highwayman'	• Comprehension Skills Pupil Book 6, Unit 7, pages 26–29 • Comprehension Skills Teacher's Guide 6 – Unit 7, pages 40–42 – Photocopiable Unit 7, Resource 1: Three diaries, page 100 – Photocopiable Unit 7, Resource 2: The highwayman's character, page 101	Collins Connect Treasure House Comprehension Year 6, Unit 7
8	Non-fiction (news report): Save it!	• Comprehension Skills Pupil Book 6, Unit 8, pages 33–36 • Comprehension Skills Teacher's Guide 6 – Unit 8, pages 45–47 – Photocopiable Unit 8, Resource 1: Latest news, page 102 – Photocopiable Unit 8, Resource 2: Alternative solutions, page 103	Collins Connect Treasure House Comprehension Year 6, Unit 8
9	Non-fiction (information text): Deserts	• Comprehension Skills Pupil Book 6, Unit 9, pages 37–40 • Comprehension Skills Teacher's Guide 6 – Unit 9, pages 48–50 – Photocopiable Unit 9, Resource 1: Desert animals, page 104 – Photocopiable Unit 9, Resource 2: Continuing 'Deserts', page 105	Collins Connect Treasure House Comprehension Year 6, Unit 9
10	Poetry: Views of winter	• Comprehension Skills Pupil Book 6, Unit 10, pages 41–43 • Comprehension Skills Teacher's Guide 6 – Unit 10, pages 51–53 – Photocopiable Unit 10, Resource 1: Painting a picture, page 106 – Photocopiable Unit 10, Resource 2: Similes and metaphors, page 107	Collins Connect Treasure House Comprehension Year 6, Unit 10
11	Fiction: 'The Phantom Tollbooth'	• Comprehension Skills Pupil Book 6, Unit 11, pages 44–47 • Comprehension Skills Teacher's Guide 6 – Unit 11, pages 54–56 – Photocopiable Unit 11, Resource 1: About the boy, page 108 – Photocopiable Unit 11, Resource 2: Idioms, page 109	Collins Connect Treasure House Comprehension Year 6, Unit 11
12	Fiction (classic): 'The Railway Children'	• Comprehension Skills Pupil Book 6, Unit 12, pages 48–51 • Comprehension Skills Teacher's Guide 6 – Unit 12, pages 57–59 – Photocopiable Unit 12, Resource 1 Ruth's diary, page 110 – Photocopiable Unit 12, Resource 2: Hiding the truth, page 111	Collins Connect Treasure House Comprehension Year 6, Unit 12

Unit	Title	Treasure House Resources	Collins Connect

13	Fiction (classic): 'Gulliver's Travels'	• Comprehension Skills Pupil Book 6, Unit 13, pages 52–55
		• Comprehension Skills Teacher's Guide 6
		  – Unit 13, pages 60–62
		  – Photocopiable Unit 13, Resource 1: Gulliver's comic strip, page 112
		  – Photocopiable Unit 13, Resource 2: A strange language, page 113
			Collins Connect Treasure House Comprehension Year 6, Unit 13

14	Playscript: 'Compere Lapin and Compere Tig'	• Comprehension Skills Pupil Book 6, Unit 14, pages 56–59
		• Comprehension Skills Teacher's Guide 6
		  – Unit 14, pages 63–65
		  – Photocopiable Unit 14, Resource 1: Finding the features, page 114
		  – Photocopiable Unit 14, Resource 2: A new trick, page 115
			Collins Connect Treasure House Comprehension Year 6, Unit 14

15	Non-fiction (autobiography): 'Wild Swans'	• Comprehension Skills Pupil Book 6, Unit 15, pages 63–66
		• Comprehension Skills Teacher's Guide 6
		  – Unit 15, pages 68–70
		  – Photocopiable Unit 15, Resource 1: Questions about China, page 116
		  – Photocopiable Unit 15, Resource 2: Researching China, page 117
			Collins Connect Treasure House Comprehension Year 6, Unit 15

16	Poetry: 'Rebecca (Who Slammed Doors for Fun and Perished Miserably)'	• Comprehension Skills Pupil Book 6, Unit 16, pages 67–69
		• Comprehension Skills Teacher's Guide 6
		  – Unit 16, pages 71–73
		  – Photocopiable Unit 16, Resource 1: Poem pieces, page 118
		  – Photocopiable Unit 16, Resource 2: Poem planner, page 119	

17	Fiction (modern): 'Project Bright Spark'	• Comprehension Skills Pupil Book 6, Unit 17, pages 70–72
		• Comprehension Skills Teacher's Guide 6
		  – Unit 17, pages 74–76
		  – Photocopiable Unit 17, Resource 1: Briony's character, page 120
		  – Photocopiable Unit 17, Resource 2: Bright Spark storyboard, page 121	

18	Fiction: 'The 39 Steps'	• Comprehension Skills Pupil Book 6, Unit 18, pages 73–75
		• Comprehension Skills Teacher's Guide 6
		  – Unit 18, pages 77–79
		  – Photocopiable Unit 18, Resource 1: Making decisions, page 122
		  – Photocopiable Unit 18, Resource 2: Timeline, page 123	

Unit	Title	Treasure House Resources	Collins Connect

19	Non-fiction (autobiography): 'Benjamin Zephaniah: My Story'	• Comprehension Skills Pupil Book 6, Unit 19, pages 76–78
		• Comprehension Skills Teacher's Guide 6
		  – Unit 19, pages 80–82
		  – Photocopiable Unit 19, Resource 1: Fact or opinion? page 124
		  – Photocopiable Unit 19, Resource 2: Planning a lesson, page 125	

20	Non-fiction (information text): 'The Kingdom of Benin'	• Comprehension Skills Pupil Book 6, Unit 20, pages 79–81
		• Comprehension Skills Teacher's Guide 6
		  – Unit 20, pages 83–85
		  – Photocopiable Unit 20, Resource 1: Quick quiz, page 126
		  – Photocopiable Unit 20, Resource 2: Researching West Africa, page 127	

Unit 1: Fiction: 'Trouble Half-Way'

Overview

English curriculum objectives

- Continue to read and discuss an increasingly wide range of fiction, poetry, plays, non-fiction and reference books or textbooks
- Increase their familiarity with a wide range of books, including myths, legends and traditional stories, modern fiction, fiction from our literary heritage, and books from other cultures and traditions
- Recommend books that they have read to their peers, giving reasons for their choices
- Identify and discuss themes and conventions in and across a wide range of writing
- Make comparisons within and across books
- Check that the book makes sense to them, discussing their understanding and exploring the meaning of words in context
- Ask questions to improve their understanding
- Draw inferences such as inferring characters' feelings, thoughts and motives from their actions, and justifying inferences with evidence
- Predict what might happen from details stated and implied
- Identify how language, structure and presentation contribute to meaning
- Discuss and evaluate how authors use language, including figurative language, considering the impact on the reader
- Participate in discussions about books that are read to them and those they can read for themselves, building on their own and others' ideas and challenging views courteously
- Explain and discuss their understanding of what they have read, including through formal presentations and debates, maintaining a focus on the topic and using notes where necessary
- Provide reasoned justification for their views

Treasure House resources

- Comprehension Skills Pupil Book 6, Unit 1, pages 4–7
- Collins Connect Treasure House Comprehension Year 6, Unit 1
- Photocopiable Unit 1, Resource 1: Amy's character, page 88
- Photocopiable Unit 1, Resource 2: Richard's view, page 89

Additional resources

- Dictionaries or the internet (optional)
- *Trouble Half-Way* by Jan Mark, whole text (optional)

Introduction

Teaching overview

Trouble Half-Way is a story about the perceptions of the main character, Amy, and her developing relationship with her stepfather. It encourages children to draw inferences regarding characters' feelings, thoughts and motives from their actions, and to justify inferences with evidence. There are opportunities to develop children's ability to evaluate how authors use language to portray characters' feelings, thoughts and motives, considering the impact on the reader.

Introduce the extract

Ask the children if any of them know the story *Trouble Half-Way*. If they do, invite them to share their knowledge with the class.

Tell the children that in this lesson they will focus on one extract from the story. Then they will answer questions about the extract. Remind children that sometimes the answers to the questions will be clearly written in the extract, but that sometimes they may need to think a little harder and use their own ideas, supported by the text.

Ask the children to read the extract individually or in pairs. Ask them to note down any words they do not understand. Discuss unknown or unusual vocabulary before setting children to work answering the questions in the Pupil Book. Try to avoid discussing the content of the extract until after the children have answered the Pupil Book questions.

Unit 1: Fiction: 'Trouble Half-Way'

Pupil practice

Pupil Book pages 6–7

Get started

Ask children to write sentences to answer the questions, using quotations where possible.
Suggested answers:

1. Amy didn't want to call Richard 'Step-Daddy' because she thought it 'sounded daft'. [1 mark]
2. Mum said she ironed the nappies because 'it looks … nicer' (and that she 'can see them', even if no one else can). [1 mark]
3. Amy's sister is called Helen. [1 mark]
4. Amy has hurt her knee: there is an 'elastic bandage around Amy's knee'. [1 mark]
5. The stretchy part of Amy's socks was giving way 'because she kept tugging at them during lessons'. [1 mark]
6. Debra 'turned her ankle on the beam on Wednesday. She came down too heavy'. [1 mark]
7. Amy's teacher is called Miss Oxley. [1 mark]
8. Amy's mum suggests she write a note to the teacher to request that Amy be let 'off games and that for the start of next week', because she thinks Amy should 'be careful' as she wants her knee to be 'right for Thursday'. [1 mark]

Try these

Ask children to write sentences to answer the questions, explaining their answers as fully as they can. The children's answers may be subjective but should be in their own words and well justified, using evidence from either the text or the children's own experiences. **Possible answers:**

1. Answers could detect that Amy's mum saying 'You never called your dad Michael, did you?' suggests that Amy's dad and Richard are or should be equals in Amy's eyes. Amy's dad, Michael, has died; this is therefore a particularly sensitive subject for Amy. [2 marks]
2. Answers could suggest that Amy's mum may not have liked Amy calling Richard by his name because it seems too impersonal for someone who is a family member, or too like a friend for someone who has become a parental figure. [2 marks]
3. Answers should infer that Amy's sister is a baby as the extract refers to her mum ironing nappies. [2 marks]
4. Answers could detect Amy's sense of duty, formality and awkward politeness towards Richard, the idea that she may not feel (or want to feel) comfortable enough to be more relaxed around him, and her consciousness that her mum is judging (and may criticise) the way she behaves towards him. [2 marks]
5. Answers should refer to Amy's need to practise something in games and her teacher's assertion that she's 'the best chance we've got if Debra isn't better'. They should conclude that Amy's leg needs to recover for a sports competition on Thursday, perhaps gymnastics (Debra 'turned her ankle on the beam'). [2 marks]
6. Answers should refer to Amy's mum's sharp response to the suggestion Amy's leg hurt ('What do you mean, not too bad?' Mum said, quickly. 'Has it been hurting?'), her command that Amy 'be careful' and her offer to write Amy a note to let her off games in the run-up to the event on Thursday. [2 marks]
7. Answers could speculate that Richard seems perplexed about Amy kneeling in assembly, and that this question shows his surprise at the idea she prays at school. They could also suggest that the wording of the question shows that Richard was either too surprised to structure it formally, or that he is joking about the idea of kneeling to pray. [2 marks]
8. Answers could refer to the tension between Amy and Richard, the presence of a baby, Amy's injury and the importance of the event happening on Thursday, and perhaps the continued feelings of loss regarding her first husband. [2 marks]

Now try these

The children's answers will be subjective, but should be well justified where appropriate. **Possible answers:**

1. Answers could refer to Amy's discomfort with Richard, her feelings about her mother's unfairness, her habit of tugging at her socks during class (perhaps revealing a lack of academic interest), her talent at sport and/or her commitment to her team. [3 marks max]
2. Answers could include the image of Amy's mum repeatedly ironing nappies and socks; the memory of her snapping 'unreasonably' at Amy about what she calls Richard; the words/phrases: 'Mum did not like her calling him Richard', 'Mum was folding the napkins into even smaller squares', 'Mum would retort', 'Mum was looking at her socks but not saying anything', '"What do you mean, not too bad?" Mum said quickly', or the sarcasm of '"What did you do in assembly, then?" Mum demanded, unfolding the ironing board. "Stand on one leg?"' [3 marks max]
3. Answers could refer to Richard teasing Amy's mum about ironing the nappies; his assertion that 'life's too short' to worry about them; his apparent concern for Amy's knee; his surprise at her praying at school; and/or the jokey way he questions her about it. [3 marks max]

Unit 1: Fiction: 'Trouble Half-Way'

4. Answers should acknowledge that the tense of this section is different (it is conditional rather than past): 'Richard would ask, sometimes', 'Mum would say', 'Mum would retort', 'Richard would be looking at the laundry basket', 'he would say'. This contrasts with the next section: 'Now he was looking at the elastic bandage around Amy's knee'.
[3 marks max]

5. Open-ended question: Look for relevance to task, consistency of character and theme, imagination and presentation. [3 marks max]

Support, embed & challenge

Support
Use Unit 1 Resource 1: Amy's character to support children in exploring the character of Amy further. Children should reread the text carefully to extract information that they can use in the profile. If the information isn't easily located in the extract, discuss with the children what the answers could be, encouraging them to infer ideas from the text and expand their own thoughts about Amy.

Embed
Use Unit 1 Resource 2: Richard's view to encourage children to consider Richard's thoughts and feelings throughout the extract. Children should retell the extract as a conversation between Richard and his sister, thinking about Richard's point of view throughout.

Challenge
The extract mentions a conversation between Amy and her mum about what Amy should call Richard. Ask children to write the part of the story that features that conversation. Is Richard there too? Ask them to think carefully about how they can show the characters' feelings and opinions through the things they say and the way they respond to one another.

Homework / Additional activities

What happens next?
Ask children to write the next part of the story using information from the extract (Amy's knee injury and Debra's ankle; the event on Thursday) and their imagination. Remind them that their extension should be in keeping with the characters' personalities and feelings.

Collins Connect: Unit 1
Ask the children to complete Unit 1 (see Teach → Comprehension → Year 6 → Unit 1).

Unit 2: Fiction (traditional): 'The Discontented Fish'

Overview

English curriculum objectives

- Continue to read and discuss an increasingly wide range of fiction, poetry, plays, non-fiction and reference books or textbooks
- Increase their familiarity with a wide range of books, including myths, legends and traditional stories, modern fiction, fiction from our literary heritage, and books from other cultures and traditions
- Recommend books that they have read to their peers, giving reasons for their choices
- Identify and discuss themes and conventions in and across a wide range of writing
- Make comparisons within and across books
- Check that the book makes sense to them, discussing their understanding and exploring the meaning of words in context
- Ask questions to improve their understanding
- Draw inferences such as inferring characters' feelings, thoughts and motives from their actions, and justifying inferences with evidence
- Predict what might happen from details stated and implied
- Identify how language, structure and presentation contribute to meaning
- Discuss and evaluate how authors use language, including figurative language, considering the impact on the reader
- Participate in discussions about books that are read to them and those they can read for themselves, building on their own and others' ideas and challenging views courteously
- Explain and discuss their understanding of what they have read, including through formal presentations and debates, maintaining a focus on the topic and using notes where necessary
- Provide reasoned justification for their views

Treasure House resources

- Comprehension Skills Pupil Book 6, Unit 2, pages 8–11
- Collins Connect Treasure House Comprehension Year 6, Unit 2
- Photocopiable Unit 2, Resource 1: The little big comic strip, page 90
- Photocopiable Unit 2, Resource 2: Morals, page 91

Additional resources

- Dictionaries or the internet (optional)

Introduction

Teaching overview

The Discontented Fish is a tale about a fish who is unsatisfied with his life, as he arrogantly believes he is better than his peers. He goes to find a grander home but, when he gets there, he realises the value of his original community. He returns and is therefore a more appreciative fish. The moral of the story is to appreciate, with modesty, what you have. This version originates from Senegal in West Africa but is representative of many similar traditional tales with the same message. A folk tale is a story originating in popular culture, typically passed on by word of mouth. *The Discontented Fish* is a type of folk tale called a 'fable'. A fable is a short story, typically with animals as characters, conveying a moral.

Introduce the text

Ask the children if they have heard of or know anything about the country Senegal. If they do, invite them to share their knowledge with the class.

Tell the children that in this lesson they will focus on a traditional folk story from Senegal that conveys a moral that applies across any culture. Ask them to think about what the moral might be during their reading, and to be prepared to share their ideas afterwards. Then they will answer questions about the text. Remind children that sometimes the answers to the questions will be clearly written in the fable, but that sometimes they may need to think a little harder and use their own ideas, supported by the text.

Ask the children to read the text individually or in pairs. Ask them to note down any words they do not understand. Discuss unknown or unusual vocabulary before setting children to work answering the questions in the Pupil Book. Try to avoid discussing the content of the fable until after the children have answered the Pupil Book questions.

25

Unit 2: Fiction (traditional): 'The Discontented Fish'

Pupil practice

Pupil Book pages 10–11

Get started
Ask children to write sentences to answer the questions, using quotations where possible.
Suggested answers:

1. The small pool is described as 'a still, muddy pool, stony and weedy, and surrounded by scraggy trees and bushes'. [1 mark]
2. The little big fish 'kept himself to himself. He was aloof and haughty whenever the others came near him'. [1 mark]
3. The older fish 'was becoming irritated by the big fish's constant gripes'. [1 mark]
4. The little big fish decided he would allow himself 'to be swept down into the big river and out of this little pool'. [1 mark]
5. The little big fish needed rain and floods for his plan to work. [1 mark]
6. When he reached the river, the little big fish sighed 'with anticipation of the good life that lay ahead'. [1 mark]
7. The little big fish got away from the black and white fish by wedging himself 'into a crevice in the bank, just out of their reach'. [1 mark]
8. The little big fish got back to the small pool 'with a leap… into the expanse of flood-water' and then by swimming 'against the swirling torrent'. [1 mark]

Try these
Ask children to write sentences to answer the questions, explaining their answers as fully as they can. The children's answers may be subjective but should be in their own words and well justified, using evidence from either the text or the children's own experiences. **Possible answers:**

1. Answers should explain that the little big fish 'kept himself to himself. He was aloof and haughty whenever the others came near him'. [2 marks]
2. Answers should refer to the little big fish thinking 'how much too big and important he was to be living in such a small pool' and the older fish's (sarcastic) suggestion that he go 'off to the big river and mix with the other big and important fish'. [2 marks]
3. Answers should refer to the fact that the little big fish calls the older fish 'my friend'. [2 marks]
4. Answers should refer to the fact that the little big fish thinks of the older fish as a friend despite the fact that the older fish is 'irritated' by him and speaks to him 'sarcastically'. [2 marks]
5. Answers should refer to the little big fish's anticipation of a 'good life' where he is able to mix with his 'equals' and live 'among fish of my own size, beauty and intelligence'. [2 marks]
6. Answers should refer to the little big fish being told: 'Out of the way, little fellow! Don't you know this is our hunting ground?' [2 marks]
7. Answers should refer to the river being full of larger fish who are rude to the little big fish or who want to eat him. [2 marks]
8. Answers should refer to the little big fish's decision to return to the safety of the small pool rather than stay in the river, for example: *He learned he would rather be a big fish in a small pond than a small fish in a big river.* [2 marks]

Now try these
The children's answers will be subjective, but should be well justified where appropriate. **Possible answers:**

1. Answers could refer to the little big fish's initial rudeness and elitism, his ambition and hopes about the big river, his joy at arriving there, his confusion and fear at the reality of the river, his decision to return to the pool, his struggle to get there and/or his relief at being back. [3 marks max]
2. Answers could refer to the older fish's irritation, sarcasm, manipulation of the little big fish into leaving and/or solemnness when congratulating the little big fish on 'his' idea. [3 marks max]
3. Answers should grasp that this is the moment the little big fish begins to doubt himself and the wisdom of moving to the river. [3 marks max]
4. The phrase describes the little big fish's return to the pool. Answers could refer to the strength of the description created by the words 'struggled', 'force' and 'swirling torrent' when building up a picture of the homeward journey. They could suggest that the difficulty of this journey proves how desperate the little big fish is to return to the pool. [3 marks max]
5. Open-ended question: Look for the relevance to the plot and characters established, and correct punctuation of dialogue. The story's moral could refer to being content with one's circumstances / not being arrogant about one's better qualities / realising there are always people better off, and should acknowledge that the little big fish rejects the challenging world of the river in favour of safety and familiarity. [3 marks max]

Unit 2: Fiction (traditional): 'The Discontented Fish'

Support, embed & challenge

Support
Use Unit 2 Resource 1: The little big comic strip to support children in exploring the plot of the story. Ask children to retell the story using a comic strip layout and style. Support them to think about how they will divide the story into the number of boxes given in the comic strip template, and how they will use the thought and speech bubbles. Support children to summarise each scene to retell the story using minimal words.

Embed
Use Unit 2 Resource 2: Morals to encourage children to consider the concept of stories that have morals. Ask children to try to explain the morals. They should discuss them in groups or research them further. You could then encourage them to choose one moral around which to write a fable of their own.

Challenge
Ask children to think carefully about the moral of the story. Ask them to write their own short story based on this moral or a similar one, but using human characters instead of animals. Ask: 'What might your main character learn during your story?'

Homework / Additional activities

More morals
Ask the children to research other stories with morals similar to that in *The Discontented Fish*. The children could also be asked to present or share the stories they find with small groups or the whole class.

Collins Connect: Unit 2
Ask the children to complete Unit 2 (see Teach → Comprehension → Year 6 → Unit 2).

Unit 3: Non-fiction (persuasive writing): Advertisements

Overview

English curriculum objectives

- Continue to read and discuss an increasingly wide range of fiction, poetry, plays, non-fiction and reference books or textbooks
- Read books that are structured in different ways and read for a range of purposes
- Identify and discuss themes and conventions in and across a wide range of writing
- Check that the book makes sense to them, discussing their understanding and exploring the meaning of words in context
- Ask questions to improve their understanding
- Summarise the main ideas drawn from more than one paragraph, identifying key details that support the main idea
- Identify how language, structure and presentation contribute to meaning
- Distinguish between statements of fact and opinion
- Retrieve, record and present information from non-fiction
- Participate in discussions about books that are read to them and those they can read for themselves, building on their own and others' ideas and challenging views courteously
- Explain and discuss their understanding of what they have read, including through formal presentations and debates, maintaining a focus on the topic and using notes where necessary
- Provide reasoned justification for their views

Treasure House resources

- Comprehension Skills Pupil Book 6, Unit 3, pages 12–14
- Collins Connect Treasure House Comprehension Year 6, Unit 3
- Photocopiable Unit 3, Resource 1: Bike advert, page 92
- Photocopiable Unit 3, Resource 2: Bike questionnaire, page 93

Additional resources

- Dictionaries or the internet (optional)
- Examples of advertisements in leaflets or from magazines (optional)

Introduction

Teaching overview

In this unit, children are able to explore the purpose and effective features of advertisements. They will be encouraged to think about who the intended reader of the advertisements is and how the language, structure and presentation of the text can influence engagement with it. Providing a wide selection of advertisements gathered from magazines and leaflets could enhance the lesson by stimulating broader discussion beforehand or afterwards.

Introduce the texts

Ask the children what advertisements are, what their purpose is and where we can see them. Hold a general discussion about adverts to elicit that they are a form of persuasive text. Tell the children that in this lesson they will focus on two different adverts about the same product. Then they will answer questions about them. Remind children that sometimes the answers to the questions will be clearly written in the text, but that sometimes they may need to think a little harder and use their own ideas, supported by the text.

Ask the children to read the adverts individually or in pairs. Ask them to note down any words they do not understand. Discuss unknown or unusual vocabulary before setting children to work answering the questions in the Pupil Book. Try to avoid discussing the content of the adverts until after the children have answered the Pupil Book questions.

Pupil practice

Pupil Book pages 13–14

Get started

Ask children to write sentences to answer the questions, using quotations where possible. **Suggested answers:**

1. Both of these adverts are promoting a new kind of trainers, or 'sports shoe'. [1 mark]
2. The brand name of the product is 'Strobers'. [1 mark]
3. You can buy the trainers 'in your favourite store' / 'from all major department stores and good sports shops'. [1 mark]
4. The trainers have 'maximum grip all rubber soles', 'strong tops and laces' and come in the 'latest colour range'. [1 mark]
5. James from Express says: 'Strobers, they're cool and canny'. [1 mark]
6. According to the adverts, 'the seriously sporty', and people who 'run, jump, kick or just look cool' will want to buy Strobers. [1 mark]
7. The trainers cost from £39.99 to £70 (Advert 1 says 'from only £39.99'; Advert 2 says 'price £40–£70 per pair'). [1 mark]
8. The colours used on Advert 1 are mostly red, black and white (orange, blue and brown are also used). The colours used on Advert 2 are pale blue and black. [1 mark]

Try these

Ask children to write sentences to answer the questions, explaining their answers as fully as they can. The children's answers may be subjective but should be in their own words and well justified, using evidence from either the text or the children's own experiences. **Possible answers:**

1. Answers could suggest that people who like that celebrity will be more likely to like the trainers, and/or that a 'cool' celebrity will make the trainers appear 'cool'. [2 marks]
2. Answers should mention that fans of James may want to copy him / take his advice by buying the trainers, and will also get a free poster of him when they do. [2 marks]
3. Answers should refer to the advert suggesting that the trainers may sell out ('while stocks last') and that the 'special introductory price' may expire, and to the advert wanting to create a sense of urgency so people will buy the trainers quickly. [2 marks]
4. Answers should refer to the word 'Strobers' being a logo in Advert 1 (it is red, in a different and larger font to the rest of the text and the final letter 's' has been used to create a line underneath the word). [2 marks]
5. Answers could refer to the fonts and colours breaking up the text to make it clearer and easier to read, making key points such as the price stand out and attracting the viewer's attention. [2 marks]
6. Answers should acknowledge that the 'from only £39.99' price shown in Advert 1 is more likely to attract customers because it gives the impression of being cheaper (even though it is only a penny cheaper than the £40 price being given on Advert 2). [2 marks]
7. Answers should refer to the advert's efforts to make the trainers appeal to those who do sports as well as those who 'just look cool'. [2 marks]
8. Open-ended question: Look for answers that are well justified and explain the choice made. (Justifications for Advert 2 could include clarity, simplicity and lack of manipulation.) [2 marks]

Now try these

The children's answers will be subjective, but should be well justified where appropriate. **Possible answers:**

1. Answers should grasp that facts are true and certain, whereas opinions are personal beliefs or judgements. [2 marks]
2. Facts could include the trainers' features ('maximum grip all rubber soles', 'strong tops or laces', 'latest colour range'), where they can be bought ('from all major department stores and good sports shops'), their price (from £39.99), and the fact that buyers 'this month' get a 'free James poster'). All other features of the advert are opinions. [3 marks max]
3. Open-ended question: Look for explanations of how the language is persuasive and intended to make the trainers appealing to buyers. [3 marks max]
4. Open-ended question: Answers could suggest adding eye-catching images, fonts, colours, features, offers and/or endorsements. [3 marks max]
5. Open-ended questions: Look for relevance to task and the character described, details from the adverts, persuasive language, imagination and presentation. [3 marks max]

Unit 3: Non-fiction (persuasive writing): Advertisements

Support, embed & challenge

Support
Use Unit 3 Resource 1: Bike advert to support children in further exploring the features used in a persuasive advert. Ask children to use highlighter pens to identify features that are similar to those seen in the Strobers advert, and then to discuss them. You could also discuss how the advert could be improved, and children could redesign the advert themselves – adding, for example, better descriptions or using more powerful language.

Embed
Use Unit 3 Resource 2: Bike questionnaire to encourage children to think about what would persuade people to buy a new bike. They should begin with the open question, 'What would persuade you to buy this bike?', and then ask a series of more specific questions, for example: *What is more important to you, the appearance of the bike or its features?* They could then share the information they have gathered with a group or the class.

Challenge
Ask pairs to improvise a TV advert for Strobers trainers. Ask: 'What information will you include?', 'Will you show a scene featuring people wearing the trainers, or might a presenter be talking straight to the camera?' Ask children to create a storyboard for their advert, and also to write it as a playscript.

Homework / Additional activities

Adding adverts
Ask children to research and collect examples of adverts at home. Ask them to make a note of where they found the adverts and who they think the intended audience is.

Collins Connect: Unit 3
Ask the children to complete Unit 3 (see Teach → Comprehension → Year 6 → Unit 3).

Unit 4: Non-fiction (emails): Climate change, what climate change?

Overview

English curriculum objectives

- Continue to read and discuss an increasingly wide range of fiction, poetry, plays, non-fiction and reference books or textbooks
- Read books that are structured in different ways and read for a range of purposes
- Identify and discuss themes and conventions in and across a wide range of writing
- Check that the book makes sense to them, discussing their understanding and exploring the meaning of words in context
- Ask questions to improve their understanding
- Summarise the main ideas drawn from more than one paragraph, identifying key details that support the main idea
- Identify how language, structure and presentation contribute to meaning
- Distinguish between statements of fact and opinion
- Retrieve, record and present information from non-fiction
- Participate in discussions about books that are read to them and those they can read for themselves, building on their own and others' ideas and challenging views courteously
- Explain and discuss their understanding of what they have read, including through formal presentations and debates, maintaining a focus on the topic and using notes where necessary
- Provide reasoned justification for their views

Treasure House resources

- Comprehension Skills Pupil Book 6, Unit 4, pages 15–18
- Collins Connect Treasure House Comprehension Year 6, Unit 4
- Photocopiable Unit 4, Resource 1: For and against, page 94
- Photocopiable Unit 4, Resource 2: An email to Pete, page 95

Additional resources

- Dictionaries or the internet (optional)

Introduction

Teaching overview

The main source text is a series of eight short, fictional emails between Josh (a fictional school boy) and his grandfather. Josh writes in an informal style to ask his grandfather for advice regarding a school project on climate change. Subsequently, Josh and his grandfather debate the arguments for and against the existence and cause of climate change. The emails provide an opportunity to explore the degrees of formality or informality that may be required when emailing different recipients, as well as giving information about climate change and the opinions that surround it.

Introduce the text

Ask the children if they use email, how often, and whom they email. Hold further discussion about when they think adults might use email, and the benefits of using email over posting letters and making phone calls.

Tell the children that in this lesson they will focus on a series of emails that form a conversation between a boy called Josh and his grandfather. Then they will answer questions about the text. Remind children that sometimes the answers to the questions will be clearly written in the emails, but that sometimes they may need to think a little harder and use their own ideas, supported by the text.

Ask the children to read the text individually or in pairs. Ask them to note down any words they do not understand. Discuss unknown or unusual vocabulary before setting children to work answering the questions in the Pupil Book. Try to avoid discussing the content of the emails until after the children have answered the Pupil Book questions.

Unit 4: Non-fiction (emails): Climate change, what climate change?

Pupil practice

Get started

Ask children to write sentences to answer the questions, using quotations where possible.
Suggested answers:

1. Josh's school project is 'about climate change'. [1 mark]
2. 'Grandad' is replying to Josh's emails. [1 mark]
3. One of Josh's friends said climate change is made up by journalists. (The children may conclude from later emails that this friend is Pete.) [1 mark]
4. Grandad says that without greenhouse gases 'we'd freeze, so we certainly need some'. [1 mark]
5. Pete's dad 'works for an oil company'. [1 mark]
6. Grandad says 'the next ice age isn't due here for another 10 000 years'. [1 mark]
7. Two emails were sent 'yesterday'. [1 mark]
8. According to these emails, climate change is the Earth 'warming up' 'more than it should' because 'carbon dioxide gas (and some others as well) that is produced when we burn oil and coal' 'traps the heat from the sun'; 'we must be emitting more greenhouse gases and so climate change must be taking place'. (Answers should grasp the point of this, broadly, from the emails.) [1 mark]

Try these

Ask children to write sentences to answer the questions, explaining their answers as fully as they can. The children's answers may be subjective but should be in their own words and well justified, using evidence from either the text or the children's own experiences. **Possible answers:**

1. Answers should refer to Josh hearing conflicting information about climate change from different people. [2 marks]
2. Answers may mention that the journalists 'like a good story', but should be aware that Pete is repeating information from his father. [2 marks]
3. Answers could refer to any of these assertions by Grandad:
   - 'we need to look at our planet Earth overall and over several years'
   - 'with all the gases being pumped out of cars, aircraft, power stations and so on, we must be emitting more greenhouse gases and so climate change must be taking place'
   - 'At the rate the Earth's climate and oceans are warming, the ice in the Arctic and Antarctic will have melted so much that many low-lying places will have flooded already [i.e., before 10 000 years is over]'
   - 'People who study the Earth's climate have found that as it warms up, the weather is going to get more violent and unpredictable. Hurricanes, for example, will become more powerful [...]. Deserts are increasing and places where lots of the Earth's food is grown, like the Great Plains of North America will get drier. Rain will be heavier in other parts of the world so there will be more floods. These things have already started to happen.'

   He also says that 'people who depend on other people using lots of fuel if they are to continue making money [...] don't think there is any climate change. But it doesn't make them right, does it!' [2 marks]
4. Answers could refer to any of these assertions by Josh:
   - 'it's all made up by journalists who like a good story to sell their newspapers'
   - 'it was really cold last winter'
   - 'the temperatures on Earth have always gone up and down.' [2 marks]
5. Answers should acknowledge that the specific thing that makes Grandad cross is people with a 'vested interest' in the fuel business thinking (or saying) that climate change isn't happening. [2 marks]
6. Answers should conclude that 'having a vested interest' means having a personal interest related to your own well-being / success. [2 marks]
7. Answers could mention that emails are usually shorter and more informal than letters. They do not use many features of letter form, such as writing addresses at the top of the page. [2 marks]
8. Answers should suggest that Josh is writing more informally than Grandad is, and could conclude that this is because Grandad is more used to letter form than email. [2 marks]

Now try these

The children's answers will be subjective, but should be well justified where appropriate. **Possible answers:**

1. Answers could refer to Josh wanting to listen to his friend, seeking further information when confused, his close and trusting relationship with his grandfather and/or his willingness to consider different viewpoints. [3 marks max]
2. Open-ended question: Look for relevance to task, use of the detail in the text, imagination and presentation. [3 marks max]
3. Open-ended question: Diary entries should be from Pete's point of view, and appreciate that Pete will be at least as confused as Josh: he is being given conflicting information from his father (whom he seems to trust) and at school, during the project. It is likely that Josh (his friend) will also now support the information learned at school. [3 marks max]

Pupil Book pages 17–18

Unit 4: Non-fiction (emails): Climate change, what climate change?

4. Answers could note that Grandad uses lots of exclamation marks, starts to answer his own questions and writes more informally than usual (using words and phrases such as 'Phooey!' and 'You guessed it!'). He also begins to make more personal comments about people with a 'vested interest' in denying climate change. [3 marks max]

5. Open-ended question: Look for relevance to task, consistency of characters and theme, imagination, presentation and correct punctuation of dialogue. [3 marks max]

Support, embed & challenge

Support
Use Unit 4 Resource 1: For and against to support children in extracting the arguments for and against the existence of climate change from the email exchanges between Josh and his grandfather. The children could extend this by researching further arguments more widely.

Embed
Use Unit 4 Resource 2: An email to Pete to encourage children to think about their own opinions, based on what they have read in the emails and on their own research. Ask children to write an email to Pete to explain their opinions and justifications for these, remembering to use a style of writing suitable for the medium of email.

Challenge
Ask the children to carry out some research about climate change using reference books or the internet. Then ask them to read the text again. Ask the children to use their new knowledge to help them write an email to Josh and his grandfather about what they now think. Ask: 'What could Josh tell Pete?', 'What do you think he should include in his project?'

Homework / Additional activities

Carry on questioning
Ask children to carry out their own research to answer another topical question, for example: 'Should councils build more houses or preserve green spaces?'

Collins Connect: Unit 4
Ask the children to complete Unit 4 (see Teach → Comprehension → Year 6 → Unit 4).

Unit 5: Poetry: 'Crack-a-Dawn'

Overview

English curriculum objectives

- Continue to read and discuss an increasingly wide range of fiction, poetry, plays, non-fiction and reference books or textbooks
- Identify and discuss themes and conventions in and across a wide range of writing
- Learn a wider range of poetry by heart
- Prepare poems and plays to read aloud and to perform, showing understanding through intonation, tone and volume so that the meaning is clear to an audience
- Check that the book makes sense to them, discussing their understanding and exploring the meaning of words in context
- Ask questions to improve their understanding
- Draw inferences such as inferring characters' feelings, thoughts and motives from their actions, and justifying inferences with evidence
- Identify how language, structure and presentation contribute to meaning
- Discuss and evaluate how authors use language, including figurative language, considering the impact on the reader
- Participate in discussions about books that are read to them and those they can read for themselves, building on their own and others' ideas and challenging views courteously
- Explain and discuss their understanding of what they have read, including through formal presentations and debates, maintaining a focus on the topic and using notes where necessary
- Provide reasoned justification for their views

Treasure House resources

- Comprehension Skills Pupil Book 6, Unit 5, pages 19–21
- Collins Connect Treasure House Comprehension Year 6, Unit 5
- Photocopiable Unit 5, Resource 1: Countdown summary, page 96
- Photocopiable Unit 5, Resource 2: My countdown poem, page 97

Additional resources

- Dictionaries or the internet (optional)

Introduction

Teaching overview

'Crack-a-Dawn' is a humorous narrative poem that tells the tale of a frustrated mother trying to persuade her son to get out of bed in the morning. It is a particularly good example of a poem that encourages children to draw inferences regarding characters' feelings, thoughts and motives from their actions, and to justify inferences with evidence. There are opportunities to develop children's ability to evaluate how authors use poetic language to portray characters' feelings, thoughts and motives, considering the impact on the reader.

Introduce the poem

Ask the children if they like getting up early in the mornings, or if their parents struggle to persuade them to get up. Tell the children that in this lesson they will read a poem about a boy who doesn't like getting up. Then they will answer questions about the text. Remind children that sometimes the answers to the questions will be clearly written in the poem, but that sometimes they may need to think a little harder and use their own ideas, supported by the text.

Ask the children to read the text individually or in pairs. Ask them to note down any words they do not understand. Discuss unknown or unusual vocabulary before setting children to work answering the questions in the Pupil Book. Try to avoid discussing the content of the poem until after the children have answered the Pupil Book questions.

Unit 5: Poetry: 'Crack-a-Dawn'

Pupil practice

Pupil Book pages 20–21

Get started

Ask children to write sentences to answer the questions, using quotations where possible.
Suggested answers:

1. The intended listener in the poem is Darren. [1 mark]
2. Darren's mother is speaking in the poem. She says: 'This is your mother speaking'. [1 mark]
3. The poem takes place in the 'early morning'. [1 mark]
4. It is windy and rainy outside: Darren's mum says there's 'a fresh Force Six blowing and a spot of rain lashing the rooftops'. [1 mark]
5. Darren's mum says: 'Your gerbil has been eaten by the dog'. [1 mark]
6. Darren got 20 spellings wrong in total: there were 'eighteen spellings wrong in your Geography homework' and two in the letter he forged from his father ('you could at least have spelt his Christian name right and the address'). [1 mark]
7. The poem does not say what Darren was doing on Friday afternoon. (It does suggest that he was not really at a dental appointment or at school.) [1 mark]
8. At the end of the poem, Darren's mother has started to pour tea over Darren ('I am about to pour your tea over your head […] the trickle of water you feel at this moment, is NOT an illusion'.) [1 mark]

Try these

Ask children to write sentences to answer the questions, explaining their answers as fully as they can. The children's answers may be subjective but should be in their own words and well justified, using evidence from either the text or the children's own experiences. **Possible answers:**

1. Answers should convey that 'crack-a-dawn' means 'crack of dawn', which means the very earliest hours of daylight in the morning. [2 marks]
2. Answers should conclude that Darren has been late before, referring to his mum saying 'if you want to walk [to school] again' and that he would be making her late for 'the third morning running'. [2 marks]
3. Answers should recognise that the numbers are a countdown representing the time Darren's mum is giving him to get up. [1 mark]
4. Answers should recognise both that Darren will be late for school and his mum will miss her bus if he does not hurry up. [2 marks]
5. Darren's mum suggests that the letter is from the England football team ('A letter has arrived, postmarked Wembley, inviting you to play for England next Saturday against Czechoslovakia'). [2 marks]
6. Answers should conclude that this means Darren will not be going out as he intends. [1 mark]
7. Answers could suggest that Darren was aware of the poor standard of his homework (i.e., how many spellings he had got wrong). [1 mark]
8. Answers could discuss Darren's mum's cheerful tone at the start of the poem, but also that Darren's lateness will not have come as a surprise. [2 marks]

Now try these

The children's answers will be subjective, but should be well justified where appropriate. **Possible answers:**

1. Answers should draw their conclusions from what Darren's mum says. They could refer to Darren's habitual laziness, his apparent lack of concern for his mother's job and for his gerbil, his apparent liking for international football, his inability to spell, his lack of concern for handing in homework, his dishonesty (forging the letter) and/or his truancy from school. [3 marks max]
2. True things could include the assertions that Darren's mum has brought him tea and cereal, that it is windy and rainy outside, that the bus is on time, that he got spellings wrong, that he hadn't handed in his Geography homework, that he'd forged and misspelt a letter from his father and/or that she was pouring tea over him. Untrue things, which begin after Darren's mum counts 'FIVE', could include the assertions that the gerbil has been eaten by the dog, that the dog has been eaten by a crocodile, that the crocodile is about to bite Darren's toes and/or that Darren has had a letter from the England football team. [3 marks max]
3. Answers could suggest that the countdown adds to the feel of nagging, the poem's pace and its rhythm, and helps the poem to build towards its climax. [3 marks max]
4. Answers could suggest that the long sentences also add to the feel of nagging and help to express Darren's mum's frustration with Darren. [3 marks max]
5. Open-ended question: Look for relevance to task, consistency of characters and theme, imagination and presentation. [3 marks max]

Unit 5: Poetry: 'Crack-a-Dawn'

Support, embed & challenge

Support
Use Unit 5 Resource 1: Countdown summary to support children in unpicking the things that Darren's mother says. Ask the children to look at each number in her countdown and to use their own words to summarise the point she makes after each one. The first point is given as an example.

Embed
Ask the children to imagine they have a naughty younger brother or sister. Ask them to write a poem similar to 'Crack-a-Dawn', trying to persuade their brother or sister to go to bed at night. Ask: 'What exaggerated things will you say to try and make them do what you're asking?'

Challenge
Use Unit 5 Resource 2: My countdown poem to encourage children to plan their own countdown poems. To give a little support, suggest an event to which they could count down (such as a school test or the start of a competition) and/or mind map things that could form part of the countdown with the class (such as the first news of the coming event, preparation and/or nerves).

Homework / Additional activities

What did you say?
Ask children to make notes about humorous things their parents say to them, their siblings or their pets when they are asking them to do things such as getting up in the morning, getting ready to go out and helping with chores.

Collins Connect: Unit 5
Ask the children to complete Unit 5 (see Teach → Comprehension → Year 6 → Unit 5).

Unit 6: Poetry: 'The Song of Hiawatha'

Overview

English curriculum objectives

- Continue to read and discuss an increasingly wide range of fiction, poetry, plays, non-fiction and reference books or textbooks
- Identify and discuss themes and conventions in and across a wide range of writing
- Learn a wider range of poetry by heart
- Prepare poems and plays to read aloud and to perform, showing understanding through intonation, tone and volume so that the meaning is clear to an audience
- Check that the book makes sense to them, discussing their understanding and exploring the meaning of words in context
- Ask questions to improve their understanding
- Draw inferences such as inferring characters' feelings, thoughts and motives from their actions, and justifying inferences with evidence
- Identify how language, structure and presentation contribute to meaning
- Discuss and evaluate how authors use language, including figurative language, considering the impact on the reader
- Participate in discussions about books that are read to them and those they can read for themselves, building on their own and others' ideas and challenging views courteously
- Explain and discuss their understanding of what they have read, including through formal presentations and debates, maintaining a focus on the topic and using notes where necessary
- Provide reasoned justification for their views

Treasure House resources

- Comprehension Skills Pupil Book 6, Unit 6, pages 22–25
- Collins Connect Treasure House Comprehension Year 6, Unit 6
- Photocopiable Unit 6, Resource 1: Finding the beat, page 98
- Photocopiable Unit 6, Resource 2: Hiawatha's brothers, page 99

Additional resources

- Dictionaries or the internet (optional)
- *The Song of Hiawatha* by H. W. Longfellow, whole text (optional)

Introduction

Teaching overview

This extract is part of a 22-chapter epic narrative poem called *The Song of Hiawatha*, written by Henry Longfellow in 1885. Hiawatha is a fictional character, but is loosely based on the legends of the Ojibwe and other Native American people. *The Song of Hiawatha* tells the tale of how Nokomis, Hiawatha's grandmother, taught him the ways of life, nature and the animals after his mother died in childbirth. Set in the stunning landscapes of Michigan, North America, the poem uses description, personification and repetition to create a strong example of blank verse with a clear rhythm.

Introduce the extract

Ask the children if any of them have knowledge of Native American culture. If they do, invite them to share their knowledge with the class.

Tell the children that in this lesson they will focus on one extract from a long narrative poem. Then they will answer questions about the extract. Remind children that sometimes the answers to the questions will be clearly written in the extract, but that sometimes they may need to think a little harder and use their own ideas, supported by the text.

Ask the children to read the extract individually or in pairs. Ask them to note down any words they do not understand. Discuss unknown or unusual vocabulary before setting children to work answering the questions in the Pupil Book. Try to avoid discussing the content of the extract until after the children have answered the Pupil Book questions.

Unit 6: Poetry: 'The Song of Hiawatha'

Pupil practice

Pupil Book pages 24–25

Get started

Ask children to write sentences to answer the questions, using quotations where possible.
Suggested answers:

1. Nokomis is the 'Daughter of the Moon'. [1 mark]
2. Hiawatha slept 'in his linden cradle, Bedded soft in moss and rushes'. [1 mark]
3. He was 'Safely bound with reindeer sinews'. [1 mark]
4. Nokomis called Hiawatha 'My little owlet'. [1 mark]
5. Ishkoodah was a comet 'with fiery tresses'. [1 mark]
6. The pine-trees said 'Minne-wawa!' [1 mark]
7. Hiawatha's Chickens were 'every bird'. [1 mark]
8. Hiawatha learned 'How the beavers built their lodges'. [1 mark]

Try these

Ask children to write sentences to answer the questions, explaining their answers as fully as they can. The children's answers may be subjective but should be in their own words and well justified, using evidence from either the text or the children's own experiences. **Possible answers:**

1. Answers should grasp that the poem is about the childhood of a young Native American called Hiawatha. [1 mark]
2. Answers should refer to the setting described in the first verse: the wigwam of Nokomis stands between a dark pine forest and a large body of water. The story is set in America (modern-day USA). [2 marks]
3. Answers should report that 'the whispering of the pine-trees' and 'the lapping of the water' were the 'Sound of music' to Hiawatha. They could suggest that these sounds have lyrics (of a sort) and rhythm in common with music. [2 marks]
4. Answers should give details about the rhythm: there are eight beats (syllables) and four stresses in every line (except 'Of all the beasts he learned the language' which has nine beats and four stresses). The stresses fall on beats 1, 3, 5 and 7 (beats 2, 4, 6 and 8 for the exception line). Answers could also discuss the rhythm's effect: the rhythm is regular and helps the poem to flow quickly; it could be thought to sound like drums or mimic the 'music' Hiawatha hears in the 'lapping of the water'. [2 marks]
5. Answers could suggest that the baby has no-one else to care for him and/or that Nokomis is his grandmother. (Both are true, although this is not revealed in the extract: Hiawatha's mother was Nokomis's daughter, and she has died.) [2 marks]
6. Answers should suggest that Hiawatha calls the animals his brothers because he understands them and is close to them. [1 mark]
7. Answers could suggest that Hiawatha was lonely (he is certainly alone) and/or simply that he is interested in and feels close to nature. [2 marks]
8. Answers should refer to the nature of folk and traditional tales: that they are handed down through generations, that they are used to entertain and educate and/or that they often offer fantastical explanations for things that the culture otherwise did not understand. [2 marks]

Now try these

The children's answers will be subjective, but should be well justified where appropriate. **Possible answers:**

1. Answers could refer to Nokomis's age, solitary life, love for Hiawatha, knowledge of the natural world and/or fondness for folklore and spiritual stories. [3 marks max]
2. Open-ended question: Look for seven lines from Hiawatha's point of view that mimic the style of the poem and detail something Hiawatha has learned in the forest (this could be something mentioned in the extract). [3 marks max]
3. Answers should find good examples and could suggest that the effect of the repetition is to emphasise the meaning of the repeated words, and add to the rhythmic nature of the poem. [3 marks max]
4. Answers could suggest that the word order is chosen to create the rhythm of the poem, that it creates an impression of Native American chants and/or that it enables the poet to start each line with its most important element. [3 marks max]
5. Open-ended question: Look for relevance to task, consistency of characters and theme, imagination, presentation, modern language with natural word order and no retention of other poetic devices. [3 marks max]

Support, embed & challenge

Support
Use Unit 6 Resource 1: Finding the beat to support children in familiarising themselves with the rhythm of the extract. Children should count and mark each line's syllables and beats, following the example. They could also use coloured pens and highlighters to identify instances of repetition and description.

Embed
Use Unit 6 Resource 2: Hiawatha's brothers to encourage children to think further about the nature, especially the animals, in the poem. Ask children to read the final verse again, and then to use the worksheet as they research and make brief notes about the characteristics of the animals mentioned. They could then use these notes to add more information to the final verse.

Challenge
Ask children to do some research about other Native American stories and legends. Ask them to choose one legend and then to write out part of it as a poem in the same style and rhythm as the extract.

Homework / Additional activities

The song of you
Ask children to write a poem in the same style as the extract using their own experiences of early childhood and learning new things. Ask them to think particularly about building up vivid descriptions and about how they will use rhythm.

Collins Connect: Unit 6
Ask the children to complete Unit 6 (see Teach → Comprehension → Year 6 → Unit 6).

Unit 7: Poetry: 'The Highwayman'

Overview

English curriculum objectives
- Continue to read and discuss an increasingly wide range of fiction, poetry, plays, non-fiction and reference books or textbooks
- Identify and discuss themes and conventions in and across a wide range of writing
- Learn a wider range of poetry by heart
- Prepare poems and plays to read aloud and to perform, showing understanding through intonation, tone and volume so that the meaning is clear to an audience
- Check that the book makes sense to them, discussing their understanding and exploring the meaning of words in context
- Ask questions to improve their understanding
- Draw inferences such as inferring characters' feelings, thoughts and motives from their actions, and justifying inferences with evidence
- Identify how language, structure and presentation contribute to meaning
- Discuss and evaluate how authors use language, including figurative language, considering the impact on the reader
- Participate in discussions about books that are read to them and those they can read for themselves, building on their own and others' ideas and challenging views courteously
- Explain and discuss their understanding of what they have read, including through formal presentations and debates, maintaining a focus on the topic and using notes where necessary
- Provide reasoned justification for their views

Treasure House resources
- Comprehension Skills Pupil Book 6, Unit 7, pages 26–29
- Collins Connect Treasure House Comprehension Year 6, Unit 7
- Photocopiable Unit 7, Resource 1: Three diaries, page 100
- Photocopiable Unit 7, Resource 2: The highwayman's character, page 101

Additional resources
- Dictionaries or the internet (optional)
- *The Highwayman* by Alfred Noyes, whole text (optional)

Introduction

Teaching overview
The Highwayman is a classic narrative poem set in 18th century England. It tells the story of an unnamed highwayman who is in love with Bess, a landlord's daughter. It is a good example of a poem that contains a strong rhythm and poetic devices, enabling children to discuss and evaluate how the author has used language, considering the impact on the reader.

Introduce the extract
Ask the children if any of them know the poem *The Highwayman*. If they do, invite them to share their knowledge with the class.

Tell the children that in this lesson they will focus on one extract from the poem. Then they will answer questions about the extract. Remind children that sometimes the answers to the questions will be clearly written in the extract, but that sometimes they may need to think a little harder and use their own ideas, supported by the text.

Ask the children to read the extract individually or in pairs. Ask them to note down any words they do not understand. Discuss unknown or unusual vocabulary before setting children to work answering the questions in the Pupil Book. Try to avoid discussing the content of the extract until after the children have answered the Pupil Book questions.

Unit 7: Poetry: 'The Highwayman'

Pupil practice

Pupil Book pages 28–29

Get started
Ask children to write sentences to answer the questions, using quotations where possible.
Suggested answers:

1. The highwayman approaches the inn at night. This is shown by the description in the first three lines: the wind is 'a torrent of darkness', the moon is up ('The moon was a ghostly galleon') and it is the only thing lighting the road ('The road was a ribbon of moonlight'). [2 marks]

2. The highwayman was carrying a 'pistol' (a gun) and a 'rapier' (a sword). [2 marks]

3. Bess is 'the landlord's daughter'. She is 'black-eyed', 'red-lipped', 'bonny' (pretty) and has 'long black hair'. [4 marks]

4. The highwayman 'whistled a tune to the window' to signal to Bess that he was there. [1 mark]

5. Bess was 'Plaiting a dark red love-knot into her long black hair' at the window. [1 mark]

6. Tim is an 'ostler' (a man who looks after horses) who 'loved the landlord's daughter'. [2 marks]

7. The highwayman couldn't kiss Bess because 'He scarce could reach her hand' even when he 'rose upright in the stirrups'. That is, Bess was in a window too high above him. [1 mark]

8. Instead, Bess 'loosened her hair' and let it fall over the highwayman's face and chest; 'he kissed its waves'. [1 mark]

Try these
Ask children to write sentences to answer the questions, explaining their answers as fully as they can. The children's answers may be subjective but should be in their own words and well justified, using evidence from either the text or the children's own experiences. **Possible answers:**

1. Answers should suggest that Bess doesn't want to be seen waiting for the highwayman – they could suggest that she is hiding from her father, Tim or anyone else. [1 mark]

2. Answers should suggest that the highwayman didn't want to be seen either. [1 mark]

3. Answers could repeat the poem's description of the highwayman's clothes, but should conclude that the highwayman dresses carefully and smartly (in 'lace', 'velvet' and breeches that 'fitted with never a wrinkle', and with highly-polished weapons). They could suggest that this demonstrates that the highwayman takes pride in himself – and, perhaps, does not look like a criminal. [2 marks]

4. Answers should acknowledge that the highwayman is romantically involved with Bess: he calls her his 'bonny sweetheart', asks for 'one kiss', promises to return to her and, when she lets her hair down to him, 'His face burnt like a brand'. [2 marks]

5. Open-ended question: Answers are likely to suggest that Bess is not interested in Tim. The reader is told that 'he loved the landlord's daughter', but the only other information given about him describes his appearance: in unflattering contrast with the smart highwayman, 'His face was white and peaked. His eyes were hollows of madness, his hair like mouldy hay'. [2 marks]

6. Answers should show an understanding of a highwayman's activities (robbing coaches on the road) and could refer to the highwayman saying, 'I shall be back with the yellow gold before the morning light' and the suggestion that 'they' (presumably the law) may 'harry' him (not leave him alone). [2 marks]

7. Answers should give details about the poem's structure: in the extract, there are six verses with six lines each. The number of beats (syllables) per line varies, but lines 1, 2, 3 and 6 of each verse contain six stresses each. Lines 4 and 5 contain three stresses each (with the exception of line 5 in the first verse, which contains two stresses). Lines 1 and 2 are a rhyming couplet; line 3 rhymes with line 6; lines 4 and 5 end in the same word (rhyme structure AABCCB). [2 marks]

8. Answers should grasp that the purpose of the poem is to tell the story of the highwayman and his relationship with Bess. They could expand that it intends to create very vivid pictures of the scenes in the story using powerful descriptions and repetitions. [2 marks]

Now try these
The children's answers will be subjective, but should be well justified where appropriate. **Possible answers:**

1. Answers could refer to Bess's feelings of anticipation while waiting for the highwayman, fear that they may be caught, joy when he arrives, excitement about speaking with him, longing to be able to reach him, happiness when he kisses her hair, sorrow when he leaves and worry that he will be caught. [3 marks max]

2. Answers could refer to the highwayman's pride in his appearance, dangerous lifestyle, disregard of the law, romantic nature and/or genuine feelings for Bess. [3 marks max]

3. Answers could suggest that the change of line length helps to break up the verses, and that the repetition draws the reader's attention to a key element in the picture the verse creates. [3 marks max]

Unit 7: Poetry: 'The Highwayman'

4. Metaphors: 'The wind was a torrent of darkness among the gusty trees.' / 'The moon was a ghostly galleon tossed upon cloudy seas.' / 'The road was a ribbon of moonlight over the purple moor.' Answers should grasp that these help to create a vivid picture of the moonlit scene. They could expand that the images chosen give clues about the rest of the story: 'torrent of darkness' suggests rapid and unseen movement; 'ghostly galleon tossed upon cloudy seas' suggests a dangerous journey (and death); 'ribbon' suggests a woman and recalls Bess's hair. (In the part of the poem not included in the extract, the highwayman's plans to return are reported by Tim, Bess dies trying to warn him and he dies trying to return for her.)

Similes: 'his hair like mouldy hay;' / 'Dumb as a dog he listened' / 'his face burnt like a brand'. Answers should grasp that these help to create vivid descriptions (of touch and smell): 'mouldy hay' and 'like a dog' create a very unflattering picture of Tim – that he is damp, smelly and animal-like – while 'like a brand' exaggerates the heat the highwayman feels (from blushing) when Bess's hair covers him.

Alliteration: 'Over the cobbles he clattered and clashed in the dark-inn yard' / 'He whistled a tune to the window, and who should be waiting there'. Answers should grasp that these help to create vivid descriptions of sounds: the clattering hooves on cobbles or the soft, airy whistle of the highwayman. [3 marks max]

5. Open-ended question: Look for relevance to task, consistency of characters and theme, imagination, presentation and a narrative (not poetic) style.
[3 marks max]

Support, embed & challenge

Support
Use Unit 7 Resource 1: Three diaries to support children in noticing the details in the poem, and distinguishing the three named characters. Children should write a paragraph from the points of view of the highwayman, Bess and Tim, describing the events of the night.

Embed
Use Unit 7 Resource 2: The highwayman's character to encourage children to explore the character of the highwayman further. Children should reread the text carefully to extract information that they can use in the profile. If the information isn't easily located in the extract, discuss with the children what the answers could be, encouraging them to infer ideas from the text and expand their own thoughts about the highwayman.

Challenge
Ask the children to turn their stories about what happens when the highwayman returns into a poem, with the same style and structure as the extract.

Homework / Additional activities

Amazing alliteration
Ask the children to research and find examples of effective alliteration in other poems. They should come prepared to share their examples with the class.

Collins Connect: Unit 7
Ask the children to complete Unit 7 (see Teach → Comprehension → Year 6 → Unit 7).

Review unit 1: Fiction: 'Selim-Hassan the Seventh' Book pages 30–32

Get started
Ask children to write sentences to answer the questions, using quotations where possible.

Suggested answers:

1. The men that lived in Pushnapanjipetal were notable because of their 'extreme hairiness'. [1 mark]
2. The extract says 'Selim-Hasan's father was the village barber'. [1 mark]
3. Selim-Hassan's father used 'eight swift swoops of his shining silver razor' when he shaved his customers. [1 mark]
4. The mirror is described as a 'splendid gilt-edged mirror, decorated with golden roses'. [1 mark]
5. The sons in the Selim-Hassan family history were grateful to their fathers because 'each of them in turn had practised and refined the art of shaving from twelve swift swoops of the shining silver razor to eleven, from eleven to ten, from ten to nine. Each of them in turn had passed on their skills and knowledge'. [2 marks]
6. Selim-Hassan the Seventh was different because 'he did *not* want to be a barber'. [1 mark]
7. Selim-Hassan's father felt 'anxious', and worried that his son 'takes after his great-great-great-great-grandfather' (who also did not want to be a barber). [2 marks]
8. The first Selim-Hassan 'had been a pirate'. [1 mark]

Try these
Ask children to write sentences to answer the questions, explaining their answers as fully as they can. The children's answers may be subjective but should be in their own words and well justified, using evidence from either the text or the children's own experiences.

Possible answers:

1. Answers should acknowledge that Selim-Hassan the Sixth feels proud of his heritage as a barber. He has worked hard to refine the art of shaving to eight swoops of his razor. He also takes pride in giving each customer the 'finest shave' that he has 'ever had'. [2 marks]
2. Answers could suggest that Selim-Hassan's father says Selim-Hassan the First was not a man to be proud of because he did harmful and illegal things such as 'wrecking ships'. Selim-Hassan's father says, 'It is not a good thing to be a thief.' Answers may also mention that Selim-Hassan the First was vain, as he 'collected thousands of shiny objects so that he could see his reflection any time he felt the need'. [2 marks]
3. Selim-Hassan the Seventh's behaviour in the barber's shop is ungrateful and 'positively rude'. Answers should give two examples: 'He was not in the least grateful when his father showed him how to sharpen the razors on a wetted stone'; 'He was not at all grateful when he was given the opportunity to sweep up the curls and whiskers on the shop floor' and/or 'He was positively rude when a customer asked him to pass him a hot towel.' [2 marks]
4. Answers should infer that Selim-Hassan's mother's opinion is disapproving of her son's conduct, but not without hope that he will change. This was shown when she 'rolled her eyes' and responded to her husband's worries about their son taking after the first Selim-Hassan by saying, 'I pray this isn't so'. [2 marks]
5. Answers should suggest that it is important to Selim-Hassan the Sixth for his son to become a barber because he would be upholding a long family tradition, and because Selim-Hassan the Sixth hopes his son will create a new family record for shaving customers. He says: 'Our family has been waiting for you for seven generations. You will be famous for being the first among us ever to achieve the perfect shave with only seven swift swoops of the silver razor.' [2 marks]
6. Answers could suggest that, when Selim-Hassan the Sixth 'smiled hopefully at the Seventh', he was trying to remain positive and not fall out with his son, or that he was quietly confident that he would be able to guide Selim-Hassan the Seventh to become a great barber. [2 marks]
7. Answers should suggest that the reputation of the barber's shop must have grown as the Selim-Hassans improved their technique, but that Selim-Hassan the Seventh's attitude may be causing it to decline. [2 marks]
8. Answers should detect that Selim-Hassan feels bored, frustrated, under pressure, and/or despondent because he is expected to join a profession in which he has no interest. They may also suggest that he feels curious about his ancestor Selim-Hassan the First, as he starts to ask his father questions about him. [2 marks]

Review unit 1: Fiction: 'Selim-Hassan the Seventh'

Now try these

The children's answers will be subjective, but should be well justified where appropriate.

Possible answers:

1. Answers could refer to Selim-Hassan the Seventh's difference from his ancestors, certainty of his own mind, ungratefulness towards his father, rudeness towards a customer and his curiosity about his ancestor, Selim-Hassan the First. [3 marks max]

2. Answers should acknowledge that the phrase is alliterative. They may recognise that the effect of the phrase is to create imagery in the reader's mind of the way in which the razor is swiftly and confidently moved when Selim-Hassan the Sixth is shaving his customers, partly through onomatopoeia. They may also comment that the phrase's repetition adds a rhythmic, fairy tale element to the story. [3 marks max]

3. Answers may infer that the lengthy and repeated description of the mirror emphasises its importance within the story. They may also comment that this elaborate description is in keeping with the fairy tale language used in the description of the razor's movements. [3 marks max]

4. Open-ended question: Look for relevance to task, consistency of character and theme, imagination and presentation. [3 marks max]

5. Open-ended question: Look for relevance to task, consistency of character and theme, imagination and presentation. [3 marks max]

Unit 8: Non-fiction (news report): Save it!

Overview

English curriculum objectives

- Continue to read and discuss an increasingly wide range of fiction, poetry, plays, non-fiction and reference books or textbooks
- Read books that are structured in different ways and read for a range of purposes
- Identify and discuss themes and conventions in and across a wide range of writing
- Check that the book makes sense to them, discussing their understanding and exploring the meaning of words in context
- Ask questions to improve their understanding
- Summarise the main ideas drawn from more than one paragraph, identifying key details that support the main idea
- Identify how language, structure and presentation contribute to meaning
- Distinguish between statements of fact and opinion
- Retrieve, record and present information from non-fiction
- Participate in discussions about books that are read to them and those they can read for themselves, building on their own and others' ideas and challenging views courteously
- Explain and discuss their understanding of what they have read, including through formal presentations and debates, maintaining a focus on the topic and using notes where necessary
- Provide reasoned justification for their views

Treasure House resources

- Comprehension Skills Pupil Book 6, Unit 8, pages 33–36
- Collins Connect Treasure House Comprehension Year 6, Unit 8
- Photocopiable Unit 8, Resource 1: Latest news, page 102
- Photocopiable Unit 8, Resource 2: Alternative solutions, page 103

Additional resources

- Dictionaries or the internet (optional)

Introduction

Teaching overview

'Save it!' is a news report. It presents factual information about concern over low water levels, and the news that water companies have been given three weeks to come up with plans to explain how they will respond to the shortage. Children are able to explore how language, structure and presentation contribute to the report's meaning.

Introduce the text

Invite the children to share their knowledge of the features, purpose and audience of newspaper reports.

Tell the children that in this lesson they will focus on a news report about a water shortage. Then they will answer questions about the text. Remind children that sometimes the answers to the questions will be clearly written in the report, but that sometimes they may need to think a little harder and use their own ideas, supported by the text.

Ask the children to read the report individually or in pairs. Ask them to note down any words they do not understand. Discuss unknown or unusual vocabulary before setting children to work answering the questions in the Pupil Book. Try to avoid discussing the content of the report until after the children have answered the Pupil Book questions.

Unit 8: Non-fiction (news report): Save it!

Pupil practice

Pupil Book pages 35–36

Get started

Ask children to write sentences to answer the questions, using quotations where possible.
Suggested answers:

1. The news report was written by 'Our Environment Correspondent'. [1 mark]
2. The water companies have been given 'just three weeks' to write their plans. [1 mark]
3. The plans need to show 'how they will respond to the current water shortage and to the long-term need to provide water for homes while, at the same time, protecting our rivers'. [1 mark]
4. The report says that 'leakage is the top priority' because 'an average of 30% of treated water leaks away before it can be used'. [1 mark]
5. The report says that 'the government is reversing its position on water meters'. [1 mark]
6. The report says that 'a third of domestic water goes down the toilet'. [1 mark]
7. A leaflet giving tips on how to save water has been produced by the 'Environment Agency'. [1 mark]
8. The report says that 'placing a water-filled bottle in the cistern will help by stopping the cistern from taking in so much water as it refills'. [1 mark]

Try these

Ask children to write sentences to answer the questions, explaining their answers as fully as they can. The children's answers may be subjective but should be in their own words and well justified, using evidence from either the text or the children's own experiences. **Possible answers:**

1. Answers should grasp that the news report has been produced to inform people about the water shortage and how it has led to water companies being required to produce plans to explain how they will deal with the situation. They may also suggest that the article suggests ways people can help reduce the water shortage (see below). [2 marks]
2. Answers should grasp that the report will have been intended to inform readers, and to encourage them to save water. Other effects could be that it alarms people who may either be worried about the state of the environment (for example, rivers) or concerned about the possibility they may have to install a water meter. Readers may also be pleased at the prospect of free leak repairs. [2 marks]
3. Open-ended question: Answers could suggest adding more images, sub-headings, quotes and/or other details, and/or reducing the number of bullet points so the advice is easier to absorb. [2 marks]
4. Open-ended question: Look for suggestions that are relevant to the content and tone of the article (for example a photograph of a dry, dying garden / a diagram of a water-saving tip in action, such as the bottle in the toilet cistern). [2 marks]
5. Answers should grasp that this suggestion is an opinion rather than a fact: it is in a quote by a 'water company spokesman'. [2 marks]
6. Answers should recognise that the quote adds an opinion. It also suggests a reason for installing water meters. [2 marks]
7. Answers could refer to people not knowing about leaks or ways to save water, enjoying taking baths rather than showers, needing to run washing machines or dishwashers quickly, wanting to keep their gardens watered and not wanting to use dirty water on them and/or not caring about the water shortage. [2 marks]
8. Open-ended question: Look for well-reasoned and justified opinions. [2 marks]

Now try these

The children's answers will be subjective, but should be well justified where appropriate. **Possible answers:**

1. Answers could include the headline and byline, introductory paragraph, quote from an interview, facts and figures, informative diagram, use of the passive voice, answers to What? When? Where? Who? How? and Why? questions, and short, clear sentences. [3 marks max]
2. 'Do' tips could include: place a water-filled bottle in the cistern; take showers; snoop for dripping taps and get them fixed; use washing-up water in the garden to water the flowers and vegetables; use a water butt to collect rain water for the garden; turn off the tap while you are brushing your teeth.

   'Don't' tips could include: take baths; use washing machines or dishwashers containing half loads; use fresh water in the garden to water the flowers and vegetables; run the tap while you are brushing your teeth; use sprinklers unless essential. [3 marks max]
3. Good points: people could be more aware of the water they use; people may become more conservation minded

   Bad points: the extra cost of installing meters; unfairness for people with large families; unfairness for people with medical conditions requiring frequent bathing; unfairness for people whose work makes them dirty. [3 marks max]
4. Open-ended question: Answers should include all of the points listed in the table in Question 3. Also look for relevance to task, consistency of theme, imagination and well-structured arguments. [3 marks max]
5. Open-ended question: Look for relevance to task, important information selected from the text, imagination and presentation. [3 marks max]

Support, embed & challenge

Support
Use Unit 8 Resource 1: Latest news to support children in understanding the content of the news report. Ask children to discuss what extra features have been added in the 'Water levels' report, and then to discuss them. Ask: 'Do the extra features help?', 'What effect do they have for the reader?'

Embed
Use Unit 8 Resource 2: Alternative solutions to encourage children to think more deeply about the topic. A range of more extreme solutions to water shortages are presented. Ask children to discuss the positive and negative points of each, compare them, research them further and/or to write news reports as if the government had decided to go ahead with one of the options.

Challenge
Ask the children to imagine that the water shortage has become even worse. Ask them to write another news report urging people to take water saving measures more urgently, referring to the text for information and ideas.

Homework / Additional activities

Read all about it!
Ask children to research topical events in their local newspapers. Ask them to bring an example of a news report to class and be prepared to share it with the class or a group, reading it and pointing out its features.

Collins Connect: Unit 8
Ask the children to complete Unit 8 (see Teach → Comprehension → Year 6 → Unit 8).

Unit 9: Non-fiction (information text): Deserts

Overview

English curriculum objectives

- Continue to read and discuss an increasingly wide range of fiction, poetry, plays, non-fiction and reference books or textbooks
- Read books that are structured in different ways and read for a range of purposes
- Identify and discuss themes and conventions in and across a wide range of writing
- Check that the book makes sense to them, discussing their understanding and exploring the meaning of words in context
- Ask questions to improve their understanding
- Summarise the main ideas drawn from more than one paragraph, identifying key details that support the main idea
- Identify how language, structure and presentation contribute to meaning
- Distinguish between statements of fact and opinion
- Retrieve, record and present information from non-fiction
- Participate in discussions about books that are read to them and those they can read for themselves, building on their own and others' ideas and challenging views courteously
- Explain and discuss their understanding of what they have read, including through formal presentations and debates, maintaining a focus on the topic and using notes where necessary
- Provide reasoned justification for their views

Treasure House resources

- Comprehension Skills Pupil Book 6, Unit 9, pages 37–40
- Collins Connect Treasure House Comprehension Year 6, Unit 9
- Photocopiable Unit 9, Resource 1: Desert animals, page 104
- Photocopiable Unit 9, Resource 2: Continuing 'Deserts', page 105

Additional resources

- Dictionaries or the internet (optional)

Introduction

Teaching overview

'Deserts' is an information text. It presents factual information about where deserts are located and how they are formed. Children are able to use the text to explore how language, structure and presentation contribute to meaning. The text features subheadings, paragraphs, a map and labelled diagrams.

Introduce the text

Ask the children if they have any prior knowledge of the world's deserts. If they do, invite them to share their knowledge with the class.

Tell the children that in this lesson they will focus on an information text about deserts. Then they will answer questions about the text. Remind children that sometimes the answers to the questions will be clearly written in the text, but that sometimes they may need to think a little harder and use their own ideas, supported by the text.

Ask the children to read the information text individually or in pairs. Ask them to note down any words they do not understand. Discuss unknown or unusual vocabulary before setting children to work answering the questions in the Pupil Book. Try to avoid discussing the content of the text until after the children have answered the Pupil Book questions.

Pupil practice

Pupil Book pages 39–40

Get started

Ask children to write sentences to answer the questions, using quotations where possible.

Suggested answers:

1. The text says that 'few people in the world live in inhospitable deserts'. [1 mark]
2. The text says that 'there are no hot deserts in the far north [...] of the Earth'. [1 mark]
3. The Equator is 'an imaginary line around the centre of the Earth, separating the Northern Hemisphere from the Southern Hemisphere'. [1 mark]
4. There are two hemispheres, 'the Northern Hemisphere' and 'the Southern Hemisphere'. [1 mark]
5. The text says that 'most of the major deserts lie in the two bands north and south of the Equator, along lines of latitude called the Tropic of Cancer and the Tropic of Capricorn'. [2 marks]

Unit 9: Non-fiction (information text): Deserts

6. The map shows that the Gobi Desert is in Asia. [1 mark]

7. The map shows that the Kalahari Desert is in Africa. [1 mark]

8. Some winds are very dry as they 'have already lost their water vapour because they have dropped it as rain over hills and mountains', as 'they are far from an ocean' or 'because they are very cold'. [3 marks]

Try these

Ask children to write sentences to answer the questions, explaining their answers as fully as they can. The children's answers may be subjective but should be in their own words and well justified, using evidence from either the text or the children's own experiences. **Possible answers:**

1. Answers should recognise the two subheadings as 'Where are deserts located?' and 'How are hot deserts formed?', and suggest a sensible main heading (for example: 'All about deserts' or simply 'Deserts'). [2 marks]

2. Answers should recognise that the blue arrows represent wet winds or 'Ocean winds', and that the red arrows represent inland winds or 'Dry winds'. [2 marks]

3. Answers should deduce that Death Valley must be in the North American Desert. [1 mark]

4. Answers could suggest that the map assists the reader by showing the locations and relative sizes of the world's deserts across the different continents, and that it shows their positions relative to the Equator and Tropics of Cancer and Capricorn. [2 marks]

5. Answers should deduce that the air gets water vapour from the ocean: the text says that 'cold winds blowing across cold ocean currents can't collect much water vapour' and therefore don't cause rain. [2 marks]

6. Answers should deduce from the text that lines of latitude are 'imaginary' lines around the earth: the text refers to the Tropics of Cancer and Capricorn as lines of latitude, shows them parallel with (and in the same colour and thickness as) the Equator, and states that the Equator is 'an imaginary line around the centre of the Earth'. [2 marks]

7. Answers should recognise that Africa spans both Tropics, along which 'most of the major deserts lie'. [1 mark]

8. Answers should acknowledge that people need water to survive, and could mention that the text says deserts are 'inhospitable' and that 'less harsh' weather is preferable. [1 mark]

Now try these

The children's answers will be subjective, but should be well justified where appropriate. **Possible answers:**

1. Open-ended question: Look for accurate definitions of the key or more difficult words in the text (for example: 'continent', 'desert', 'Equator', 'hemisphere' and 'inhospitable'). The words should be presented alphabetically. [3 marks max]

2. Open-ended question: Answers should be clear, numbered instructions that contain all relevant details in the text (i.e., that the wind collects water vapour from a relatively warm ocean and moves it to a cooler place to form clouds; when the water droplets become heavy, they fall as rain). [3 marks max]

3. Answers should appreciate that the diagram illustrates the sentence 'sometimes the winds bring very dry air. These winds have already lost their water vapour because they have dropped it as rain over hills and mountains'. It adds details about how and where the winds lose their water vapour and how and where 'Ocean winds' become 'Dry winds', how landscapes change the higher and further from the ocean they are, and gives a specific example of this happening: from the Pacific Ocean to Death Valley. [3 marks max]

4. Open-ended question: Answers should explain all the detail included in the diagram, including the specifics of the example (that the ocean winds collect water vapour from the Pacific Ocean; they become cooler, form clouds and drop rain over the Coast Mountains, San Joaquin Valley and Sierra Nevada Mountains; they become dry as they leave the Sierra Nevada Mountains and have no water vapour left to drop over Death Valley). [3 marks max]

5. Open-ended question: Look for relevance to task, consistency of theme, information from the text, a different structure from that used in the text, imagination and presentation. The suggested structure (that the children could start with the wind's journey from an ocean and end with an example of a desert shown on the map) may or may not be used. [3 marks max]

Unit 9: Non-fiction (information text): Deserts

Support, embed & challenge

Support
Use Unit 9 Resource 1: Desert animals to support children in understanding how specific pieces of information can be found in information texts. The children read two short passages about desert animals, and then compose three questions about each. Ask pairs to swap questions and answer each other's to check that the questions are relevant to the passages.

Embed
Use Unit 9 Resource 2: Continuing 'Deserts' to encourage children to consider further the features and composition of an information text. The children read a short passage and give it a title, before planning and researching how the text could continue.

Challenge
Ask the children to research and write a fact file about cold deserts. Ask them to include and label a world map to show where the deserts are, and to add a diagram helping you to explain how they are formed. Remind them to use a heading and subheadings, and encourage them to add one new section (perhaps about whether any wildlife lives in cold deserts).

Homework / Additional activities

Desert peoples
Ask children to research and make notes about people who live in desert regions. Ask them to be prepared to share their findings with the class in the form of a presentation.

Collins Connect: Unit 9
Ask the children to complete Unit 9 (see Teach → Year 6 → Comprehension → Unit 9).

Unit 10: Poetry: Views of winter

Overview

English curriculum objectives

- Continue to read and discuss an increasingly wide range of fiction, poetry, plays, non-fiction and reference books or textbooks
- Identify and discuss themes and conventions in and across a wide range of writing
- Learn a wider range of poetry by heart
- Prepare poems and plays to read aloud and to perform, showing understanding through intonation, tone and volume so that the meaning is clear to an audience
- Check that the book makes sense to them, discussing their understanding and exploring the meaning of words in context
- Ask questions to improve their understanding
- Draw inferences such as inferring characters' feelings, thoughts and motives from their actions, and justifying inferences with evidence
- Identify how language, structure and presentation contribute to meaning
- Discuss and evaluate how authors use language, including figurative language, considering the impact on the reader
- Participate in discussions about books that are read to them and those they can read for themselves, building on their own and others' ideas and challenging views courteously
- Explain and discuss their understanding of what they have read, including through formal presentations and debates, maintaining a focus on the topic and using notes where necessary
- Provide reasoned justification for their views

Treasure House resources

- Comprehension Skills Pupil Book 6, Unit 10, pages 41–43
- Collins Connect Treasure House Comprehension Year 6, Unit 10
- Photocopiable Unit 10, Resource 1: Painting a picture, page 106
- Photocopiable Unit 10, Resource 2: Similes and metaphors, page 107

Additional resources

- Dictionaries or the internet (optional)

Introduction

Teaching overview

'Winter Morning' by Ogden Nash is a positive, light-hearted reflection on the wonder and beauty of winter, summed up by its first line, 'Winter is the king of showmen'. 'Winter in a Wheelchair' by Emma Barnes is a poem that has many features in common with 'Winter Morning', including its seasonal theme. However, it provides a sombre and contrasting viewpoint, which is particularly powerful when read immediately after 'Winter Morning'.

Introduce the poems

Ask the children for their opinions about winter weather, and invite them to share their experiences. Discuss the positive and negative aspects of winter weather, and create two lists or mind maps on the board to show these ideas.

Tell the children that in this lesson they will focus on two short poems that give different opinions of winter. Then they will answer questions about the poems. Remind children that sometimes the answers to the questions will be clearly written in the poems, but that sometimes they may need to think a little harder and use their own ideas, supported by the text.

Ask the children to read the poems individually or in pairs. Ask them to note down any words they do not understand. Discuss unknown or unusual vocabulary before setting children to work answering the questions in the Pupil Book. Try to avoid discussing the content of the poems until after the children have answered the Pupil Book questions.

Unit 10: Poetry: Views of winter

Pupil practice

Pupil Book pages 42–43

Get started

Ask children to write sentences to answer the questions, using quotations where possible.
Suggested answers:

1. The shared topic of the poems is how people feel about winter. [1 mark]
2. Winter turns 'tree stumps into snowmen'. [1 mark]
3. Winter turns 'houses into birthday cakes'. [1 mark]
4. 'Young' people catch snowflakes on their tongues. [1 mark]
5. Snow is 'slushy when it's going'. [1 mark]
6. 'Icy tyres' scratch the young girl's hands. [1 mark]
7. Her fingers feel 'stiff and numb'. [1 mark]
8. The girl is 'alone' while watching the children playing in the snow. [1 mark]

Try these

Ask children to write sentences to answer the questions, explaining their answers as fully as they can. The children's answers may be subjective but should be in their own words and well justified, using evidence from either the text or the children's own experiences. **Possible answers:**

1. Answers should recognise that the speaker of Ogden Nash's poem feels positively about winter (for example that it is exciting/beautiful). [1 mark]
2. Answers should recognise that the speaker of Emma Barnes's poem feels negatively about winter (for example that it is lonely / it destroys her independence). [1 mark]
3. Answers should grasp that the snow prevents the girl from moving herself around freely in her wheelchair. [1 mark]
4. Answers should grasp that independence might be important to someone in a wheelchair as it is harder for them to move without people's help, and could suggest that acting without help is an important part of growing up / being your own person / having freedom / enjoying yourself. [2 marks]
5. Answers should report that, in 'Winter Morning', the rhyme pattern is five rhyming couplets (AABBCCDDEE); in 'Winter in a Wheelchair', lines 2 and 4, and lines 6 and 8 rhyme (ABCBDEFE), although lines 2 and 4 are half-rhymes ('numb' and 'sun'). [2 marks]
6. Answers could suggest that the line 'Snow is snowy when it's snowing' creates an impression of the continuous, repetitive nature of snowfall, the sounds of walking in snow and/or humour. They should recognise that the effects mentioned are created by the line's repetition (and, therefore, alliteration). [2 marks]
7. The metaphors are 'Winter is the king of showmen, / Turning tree stumps into snowmen / And houses into birthday cakes'. Answers could report that, because the metaphors suggest things actually become other things, they emphasise the transforming nature of snow in winter by likening its effects to those of a magician doing tricks. [2 marks]
8. The simile is 'My independence melts away, / Like a snowman in the sun'. Answers could suggest that the simile creates a vivid picture for an abstract concept (the independence vanishing), relates it to the topic of winter, and relates it to the feelings of disappointment other children feel at the end of winter (emphasising the speaker's alienation from them). [2 marks]

Now try these

The children's answers will be subjective, but should be well justified where appropriate. **Possible answers:**

1. Answers should accurately identify personification as the action of attributing human characteristics to non-human subjects. The example they should use from the poem is 'Winter is the king of showmen'. They could expand by detailing what effect this personification has on the poem: that winter is active, and makes transformations purposefully and magically (the metaphors that follow it emphasise the transforming nature of snow in winter by likening its effects to those of a magician doing tricks). [3 marks max]
2. The different line is 'I'm sorry it's slushy when it's going.' The change in rhythm is from four stresses per line to three stresses per line. Answers could suggest that this creates the effect of slowing down, interruption or less energy, and relate this to the end of winter and the fun described. [3 marks max]
3. The different pair of lines is 'Alone in my chair, / I watch the children play and yell'. The change in rhythm is from pairs of lines with four and then three stresses to a pair of lines with two and then four stresses. Answers could suggest that this emphasises the importance of 'Alone in my chair', which explains the real cause of the girl's unhappiness, creates the effect of interruption and/or separateness, or creates a lack of flow. They could relate this to the lack of enjoyment, movement and independence that the girl feels. [3 marks max]
4. Open-ended question: Look for relevance to task, imagination, presentation and appropriate new descriptions. Re-used positive descriptions could include any from 'Winter Morning'; re-used negative descriptions could include any from 'Winter in a Wheelchair'. [3 marks max]
5. Open-ended question: Look for relevance to task, consistency of character and theme, imagination and presentation. [3 marks max]

Unit 10: Poetry: Views of winter

Support, embed & challenge

Support
Use Unit 10 Resource 1: Painting a picture to support children in familiarising themselves with the nature of similes and metaphors. First, the children examine the examples from the poem. Then they label sentences to show whether they contain a simile or a metaphor.

[1. simile; 2. metaphor; 3. simile; 4. metaphor]

Embed
Use Unit 10 Resource 2: Similes and metaphors to encourage children to explore similes and metaphors further. The children label sentences to show whether they contain a simile or a metaphor, and then use a word bank to devise their own examples.

[1. simile; 2. metaphor; 3. simile; 4. metaphor; 5. metaphor; 6. simile]

Challenge
Ask children to make notes about positive and negative ways that they could write about summer. Using the winter poems as guides, ask the children to write two poems about summer, one from the perspective of someone who enjoys it and one from the perspective of someone who is unable to enjoy it. Encourage them to use a simile, a metaphor and an example of personification. Ask them to think carefully about how changing a line's rhythm might affect its meaning.

Homework / Additional activities

Whatever the weather
Ask children to compose their own poems to express how they feel about the current weather. Encourage them to use a simile, a metaphor and an example of personification. Ask them to think carefully about how changing a line's rhythm might affect its meaning.

Collins Connect: Unit 10
Ask the children to complete Unit 10 (see Teach → Comprehension → Year 6 → Unit 10).

Unit 11: Fiction: 'The Phantom Tollbooth'

Overview

English curriculum objectives

- Continue to read and discuss an increasingly wide range of fiction, poetry, plays, non-fiction and reference books or textbooks
- Increase their familiarity with a wide range of books, including myths, legends and traditional stories, modern fiction, fiction from our literary heritage, and books from other cultures and traditions
- Recommend books that they have read to their peers, giving reasons for their choices
- Identify and discuss themes and conventions in and across a wide range of writing
- Make comparisons within and across books
- Check that the book makes sense to them, discussing their understanding and exploring the meaning of words in context
- Ask questions to improve their understanding
- Draw inferences such as inferring characters' feelings, thoughts and motives from their actions, and justifying inferences with evidence
- Predict what might happen from details stated and implied
- Identify how language, structure and presentation contribute to meaning
- Discuss and evaluate how authors use language, including figurative language, considering the impact on the reader
- Participate in discussions about books that are read to them and those they can read for themselves, building on their own and others' ideas and challenging views courteously
- Explain and discuss their understanding of what they have read, including through formal presentations and debates, maintaining a focus on the topic and using notes where necessary
- Provide reasoned justification for their views

Treasure House resources

- Comprehension Skills Pupil Book 6, Unit 11, pages 44–47
- Collins Connect Treasure House Comprehension Year 6, Unit 11
- Photocopiable Unit 11, Resource 1: About the boy, page 108
- Photocopiable Unit 11, Resource 2: Idioms, page 109

Additional resources

- Dictionaries or the internet (optional)
- *The Phantom Tollbooth* by Norton Juster, whole text (optional)

Introduction

Teaching overview

The Phantom Tollbooth is a fascinating and unusual story about a boy called Milo and his journey through a magical fantasy world. It encourages children to draw inferences regarding characters' feelings, thoughts and motives from their actions, and to justify inferences with evidence. There are opportunities to develop children's ability to evaluate how authors use language to portray characters' feelings, thoughts and motives, considering the impact on the reader.

Introduce the extract

Ask the children if any of them know the story *The Phantom Tollbooth*. If they do, invite them to share their knowledge with the class.

Tell the children that in this lesson they will focus on one extract from the story. Then they will answer questions about the extract. Remind children that sometimes the answers to the questions will be clearly written in the extract, but that sometimes they may need to think a little harder and use their own ideas, supported by the text.

Ask the children to read the extract individually or in pairs. Ask them to note down any words they do not understand. Discuss unknown or unusual vocabulary before setting children to work answering the questions in the Pupil Book. Try to avoid discussing the content of the extract until after the children have answered the Pupil Book questions.

Unit 11: Fiction: 'The Phantom Tollbooth'

Pupil practice

Pupil Book pages 46–47

Get started

Ask children to write sentences to answer the questions, using quotations where possible. **Suggested answers:**

1. Milo thinks 'almost everything is a waste of time'. [1 mark]
2. Milo thinks that 'the magical forest of words and numbers is beautiful'. [1 mark]
3. The first thing Milo sees when he looks for the person who has spoken is 'two very neatly polished brown shoes'. [1 mark]
4. The boy's feet were 'easily three feet off the ground'. [1 mark]
5. The writer suggests that 'standing' is not the most appropriate word to describe the boy's position because he is 'suspended in mid-air'. [1 mark]
6. According to the boy Milo meets, you might not think the forest was beautiful 'if you happened to like deserts'. [1 mark]
7. Even when they are born, everyone in the boy's family is born 'with his head at exactly the same height it's going to be when he's an adult'. [1 mark]
8. The boy says that the idea someone might 'start on the ground and grow up' is a 'silly system' because 'your head keeps changing its height and you always see things a different way'. [1 mark]

Try these

Ask children to write sentences to answer the questions, explaining their answers as fully as they can. The children's answers may be subjective but should be in their own words and well justified, using evidence from either the text or the children's own experiences. **Possible answers:**

1. Answers should detect that the extract contrasts Milo's feelings that things are 'a waste of time' with his positive feelings about the forest: he feels that way 'until he mysteriously finds his way into the magical forest'. [2 marks]
2. Answers should detect that, when Milo asked, 'Isn't it beautiful?' he didn't expect anyone to answer. He was surprised to receive an answer, as he 'didn't see who had spoken'. [2 marks]
3. Answers should refer to the boy saying: 'When we're fully grown up, or as you can see, grown down, our feet finally touch. Of course, there are a few of us whose feet never reach the ground, no matter how old we get.' [2 marks]
4. Answers could include: 'We always see things from the same angle […]. It's much less trouble that way'; 'When you're very young, you can never hurt yourself falling down if you're in mid-air'; and 'you certainly can't get into trouble for scuffing up your shoes or marking the floor if there's nothing to scuff them on and the floor is three feet away'. [2 marks]
5. Answers should conclude that Milo had 'never really thought about' the fact that his head would keep 'changing its height' as he got older because that is what is normal for him, and that he hadn't considered that there might be an alternative. [2 marks]
6. Answers should detect the figurative meaning of the sentence: that some people may not think the forest is beautiful, and that the boy thinks Milo should consider different opinions. [2 marks]
7. Answers should detect the literal meaning of the sentence: that growing upwards means that your head changes height and that the angle you look at your surroundings will therefore change. [2 marks]
8. Answers should refer to the fact that, literally, Milo's view of the world will change as he grows older and gets taller, while the boy he meets will see the world from the same height. Answers should also refer to the way that, figuratively, growing up changes the way one sees the world as experience is gained and opinions change. [3 marks]

Now try these

The children's answers will be subjective, but should be well justified where appropriate. **Possible answers:**

1. Answers could refer to the boy's neat and polished shoes, his apparent open-mindedness about others' opinions, his odd changes of subject, his playful nature ('He hopped a few steps in the air, skipped back to where he started, and then began again'), his ridicule of Milo growing upwards, his assertive arguments and/or his conviction that he is right. [3 marks max]
2. Answers could refer to Milo initially thinking 'dejectedly', his awe and appreciation of the forest, his surprise at meeting the boy, his confusion at the boy's words and ability to float, the fact that he responds to the boy's misunderstanding of his age 'seriously', the fact he is asked to consider his growth system for the first time and his passive agreement with the boy. [3 marks max]
3. Open-ended question: Look for relevance to task, consistency of characters and theme, imagination and presentation. [3 marks max]
4. Open-ended question: All the boy's arguments except, perhaps, one ('if Christmas trees were people and people were Christmas trees, we'd all be chopped down, put up in the living room, and

Unit 11: Fiction: 'The Phantom Tollbooth'

covered in tinsel, while the trees opened our presents') could be counted as making sense (they aren't illogical), so answers will be subjective.

[3 marks max]

5. Open-ended question: Answers could contend that the boy does not contradict himself if his second assertion is taken literally, i.e., that he feels that you should consider other people's opinions but that seeing your surroundings from a consistent height is more productive. Alternatively, they could contend that the boy suggests, at first, that it is better to see things differently (figuratively and/or literally) and then that it is better to see things in the same way (again, figuratively and/or literally).

[3 marks max]

Support, embed & challenge

Support
Use Unit 11 Resource 1: About the boy to support children in exploring the character of the strange boy further. Children should reread the text carefully to extract information that they can use in the profile. If the information isn't easily located in the extract, discuss with the children what the answers could be, encouraging them to infer ideas from the text and expand their own thoughts about the boy.

Embed
Use Unit 11 Resource 2: Idioms to develop children's understanding of figurative language. The sheet gives a brief explanation of idioms and then provides a list of common examples. Ask children to discuss any idioms they recognise, and then to research and write an explanation of any that are unfamiliar. You may prefer the children to work in pairs or small groups, and to share out the idioms that need to be researched.

Challenge
Ask pairs to discuss the differences between literal meanings and figurative meanings. Remind them to use a dictionary if they need to. Explain that stories like the one in the extract can create interesting effects by using both literal and figurative meanings. Ask children to think of a phrase or saying that could have both kinds of meaning. If you like, you can suggest the saying 'time flies'. Ask children to write a silly short story that uses both the literal and the figurative meaning of their phrase or saying.

Homework / Additional activities

Double meanings
Ask the children to research and collect phrases or sayings that have figurative and literal meanings.

Collins Connect: Unit 11
Ask the children to complete Unit 11 (see Teach → Comprehension → Year 6 → Unit 11).

Unit 12: Fiction (classic): 'The Railway Children'

Overview

English curriculum objectives

- Continue to read and discuss an increasingly wide range of fiction, poetry, plays, non-fiction and reference books or textbooks
- Increase their familiarity with a wide range of books, including myths, legends and traditional stories, modern fiction, fiction from our literary heritage, and books from other cultures and traditions
- Recommend books that they have read to their peers, giving reasons for their choices
- Identify and discuss themes and conventions in and across a wide range of writing
- Make comparisons within and across books
- Check that the book makes sense to them, discussing their understanding and exploring the meaning of words in context
- Ask questions to improve their understanding
- Draw inferences such as inferring characters' feelings, thoughts and motives from their actions, and justifying inferences with evidence
- Predict what might happen from details stated and implied
- Identify how language, structure and presentation contribute to meaning
- Discuss and evaluate how authors use language, including figurative language, considering the impact on the reader
- Participate in discussions about books that are read to them and those they can read for themselves, building on their own and others' ideas and challenging views courteously
- Explain and discuss their understanding of what they have read, including through formal presentations and debates, maintaining a focus on the topic and using notes where necessary
- Provide reasoned justification for their views

Treasure House resources

- Comprehension Skills Pupil Book 6, Unit 12, pages 48–51
- Collins Connect Treasure House Comprehension Year 6, Unit 12
- Photocopiable Unit 12, Resource 1: Ruth's diary, page 110
- Photocopiable Unit 12, Resource 2: Hiding the truth, page 111

Additional resources

- Dictionaries or the internet (optional)
- *The Railway Children* by E. Nesbit, whole text (optional)

Introduction

Teaching overview

The Railway Children is a children's book by Edith Nesbit (1858–1924), originally printed as a serial magazine story during 1905 and first published as a book in 1906. It tells the story of three children whose lives are shattered when their father goes away with two strangers one evening. Roberta, Phyllis, Peter and their mother have to move from their comfortable London home to live in a simple country cottage, where Mother writes books to make ends meet. They soon come to love the railway that runs near their cottage, and have many adventures.

Introduce the extract

Ask the children if any of them know the story of *The Railway Children*. If they do, invite them to share their knowledge with the class.

Tell the children that in this lesson they will focus on one extract from the story. Then they will answer questions about the extract. Remind children that sometimes the answers to the questions will be clearly written in the extract, but that sometimes they may need to think a little harder and use their own ideas, supported by the text.

Ask the children to read the extract individually or in pairs. Ask them to note down any words they do not understand. Discuss unknown or unusual vocabulary before setting children to work answering the questions in the Pupil Book. Try to avoid discussing the content of the extract until after the children have answered the Pupil Book questions.

Unit 12: Fiction (classic): 'The Railway Children'

Pupil practice

Pupil Book pages 50–51

Get started

Ask children to write sentences to answer the questions, using quotations where possible. **Suggested answers:**

1. The characters in the extract are Mother, Ruth, Roberta, Phyllis and Peter. Children may also mention Father, who is discussed but does not appear in the extract. [1 mark]

2. Ruth suggests that the bad news could be 'a death in the family or a bank busted'. [1 mark]

3. When Mother returns from the library, 'Her dear face was as white as her lace collar, and her eyes looked very big and shining. Her mouth looked just like a line of pale red – her lips were thin and not their proper shape at all.' [1 mark]

4. Phyllis protests about bedtime because, she says, Mother 'promised we should sit up late tonight because Father's come home'. [1 mark]

5. Mother 'almost always' brushes the girls' hair. [1 mark]

6. In response to Peter's question, Ruth says: 'Don't ask me no questions and I won't tell you no lies.' [1 mark]

7. Mother went 'to London' in the morning. [1 mark]

8. When Mother sat down, Peter 'fetched her soft velvety slippers for her'. [1 mark]

Try these

Ask children to write sentences to answer the questions, explaining their answers as fully as they can. The children's answers may be subjective but should be in their own words and well justified, using evidence from either the text or the children's own experiences. **Possible answers:**

1. Answers could detect that Mother does not want Ruth to frighten the children with her guesses. They could also suggest that Mother does not approve of Ruth talking openly about what is happening. [2 marks]

2. Answers should conclude correctly that Ruth is a servant in the family's household. They could refer to Ruth addressing Mother with the words 'Please 'm,' or (potentially confusingly) 'Mum'; that Mother says, 'That'll do' and 'you can go' to her; and/or that she seems to have responsibility for tasks such as putting the children to bed or serving their breakfast when Mother isn't there. [2 marks]

3. Answers could suggest that Mother is upset and doesn't want a hug or, more sensitively, that she is trying to prevent Roberta from seeing her crying. They could refer to Mother's eyes being 'very big and shining' and to Roberta's realisation later that 'Mother doesn't want us to know she's been crying'. [2 marks]

4. Answers should refer to the fact that, on that night, 'Ruth brushed the girls' hair and helped them to undress' when 'Mother almost always did this herself'. They could also mention that Mother slips into the children's rooms 'late that night' to kiss them. They could conclude that Mother wanted time on her own, without the children, and that this may be because she was upset (see also previous answer). [2 marks]

5. Answers should acknowledge that Roberta is being sensitive to her mother's wish to keep her grief private and not to talk about what has happened. They could refer to Roberta thinking, 'If Mother doesn't want us to know she's been crying, […] we won't know it. That's all.' [2 marks]

6. Answers should acknowledge that the reason Mother gives for the children not to ask her questions is, 'I am very worried about it, and I want you all to help me, and not to make things harder for me.' They could also conclude that she is trying to protect them from bad news. [2 marks]

7. Answers should refer to Mother saying, 'And don't you worry. It'll all come right in the end'. They could suggest that this may reassure the children as they seem to trust and obey her, or that it will not as it hasn't answered any of the questions they may have about what happened, or told them when Father will return. [2 marks]

8. Open-ended question: Answers should refer to the mysterious upheaval in the children's lives, Mother's silence on the subject and their instructions to be good and not ask questions. They may suggest that Roberta and Peter seem more worried than Phyllis does, as her protestation about staying up late suggests that she hasn't picked up on the seriousness of the situation. [2 marks]

Now try these

The children's answers will be subjective, but should be well justified where appropriate. **Possible answers:**

1. Answers could refer to Mother's calmness and quietness despite her obviously being upset, her determined actions (such as going to London alone), her firmness with Ruth and about the children not asking questions, her protection of the children from the news and/or her kindness to the children (she allows them to 'sit up late', 'almost always' brushes the girls' hair herself and comes to kiss them goodnight). [3 marks max]

2. Answers could refer to Roberta's worry and mystification about what has happened to Father, her worry for Mother, her sensitivity to Mother's feelings and her quickness in picking up ideas (asking, after Ruth's suggestion, if anyone was dead; noticing that her Mother didn't want to talk;

Unit 12: Fiction (classic): 'The Railway Children'

correctly guessing the trouble was 'something to do with Government'). They could also mention her surprise that Mother thought they might 'make things harder' for her ('"As if we would!" said Roberta') and her 'guilty glances' with Peter when Mother mentions quarrelling. [3 marks max]

3. Answers should recognise that the dash indicates a pause. They could suggest that Mother was ready to say the first part of her sentence ('Father's been called away'), but that she had to think before adding 'on business'. They could then, correctly, expand that the second part of the sentence is not likely to be true. [3 marks max]

4. Clues could include the bad news and Ruth's suggestions that it meant a death or a 'bank busted', men in boots apparently leaving the house with Father in a cab, Mother saying 'Father's been called away – on business' (see answer above), Mother denying that anyone is dead, her grief, her trip to London, her news that 'Father will be away for some time' and that she is 'very worried about it', her saying the trouble is 'about business' and 'something to do with the Government' and her promise that 'it'll all come right in the end'. Answers could suggest anything based soundly on the selected evidence, although some ideas (such as Father's death) are contradicted by it (even if Mother weren't telling the truth, it would be unlikely that things would 'come right in the end'). (The answer, should you wish to reveal it, is that Father has been arrested for selling Government secrets – a crime of which he is eventually proved innocent.) [3 marks max]

5. Open-ended question: Look for relevance to task, consistency of character and theme, imagination and presentation. [3 marks max]

Support, embed & challenge

Support
Use Unit 12 Resource 1: Ruth's diary to support children in understanding the facts and different characters in the extract. The children write down what has happened from the perspective of Ruth, limiting their recount to what she knows and thinks.

Embed
As a class, discuss all the clues you have gathered that might help you to guess what has happened. Make a class mind map to note down all the facts, deductions and ideas. Ask: 'What do most people think has happened?', 'Does the evidence support this?' Once an agreement has been reached, ask children to work individually to add a scene to the story in which Roberta asks Mother some direct questions and Mother answers them in the way the class has decided is most likely.

Challenge
Use Unit 12 Resource 2: Hiding the truth to extend children's understanding of the character of Mother. The children track what they would do in Mother's position, imagining they have been told bad news and deciding how best to react to it.

Homework / Additional activities

Full steam ahead!
Ask children to find out more about the time period and what people thought about the earliest steam trains. Ask them to summarise what they learn and be prepared to share their findings with a group or the class.

Collins Connect: Unit 12
Ask the children to complete Unit 12 (see Teach → Comprehension → Year 6 → Unit 12).

Unit 13: Fiction (classic): 'Gulliver's Travels'

Overview

English curriculum objectives

- Continue to read and discuss an increasingly wide range of fiction, poetry, plays, non-fiction and reference books or textbooks
- Increase their familiarity with a wide range of books, including myths, legends and traditional stories, modern fiction, fiction from our literary heritage, and books from other cultures and traditions
- Recommend books that they have read to their peers, giving reasons for their choices
- Identify and discuss themes and conventions in and across a wide range of writing
- Make comparisons within and across books
- Check that the book makes sense to them, discussing their understanding and exploring the meaning of words in context
- Ask questions to improve their understanding
- Draw inferences such as inferring characters' feelings, thoughts and motives from their actions, and justifying inferences with evidence
- Predict what might happen from details stated and implied
- Identify how language, structure and presentation contribute to meaning
- Discuss and evaluate how authors use language, including figurative language, considering the impact on the reader
- Participate in discussions about books that are read to them and those they can read for themselves, building on their own and others' ideas and challenging views courteously
- Explain and discuss their understanding of what they have read, including through formal presentations and debates, maintaining a focus on the topic and using notes where necessary
- Provide reasoned justification for their views

Treasure House resources

- Comprehension Skills Pupil Book 6, Unit 13, pages 52–55
- Collins Connect Treasure House Comprehension Year 6, Unit 13
- Photocopiable Unit 13, Resource 1: Gulliver's comic strip, page 112
- Photocopiable Unit 13, Resource 2: A strange language, page 113

Additional resources

- Dictionaries or the internet (optional)
- *Gulliver's Travels* by Jonathan Swift, whole text (optional)

Introduction

Teaching overview

Gulliver's Travels is a classic English novel written by Jonathan Swift in the early 1700s. It tells of the adventures of Lemuel Gulliver as he travels to the far reaches of the world. In the extract, Gulliver's ship has been wrecked in a storm and he awakes to find himself on the island of Lilliput. He has been captured by Lilliputians, small people approximately six inches tall. The story is presented in the first person, in the form of Gulliver's travel journal.

Introduce the extract

Ask the children if any of them know the story of *Gulliver's Travels*. If they do, invite them to share their knowledge with the class.

Tell the children that in this lesson they will focus on one extract from the story. Then they will answer questions about the extract. Remind children that sometimes the answers to the questions will be clearly written in the extract, but that sometimes they may need to think a little harder and use their own ideas, supported by the text.

Ask the children to read the extract individually or in pairs. Ask them to note down any words they do not understand. Discuss unknown or unusual vocabulary before setting children to work answering the questions in the Pupil Book. Try to avoid discussing the content of the extract until after the children have answered the Pupil Book questions.

Unit 13: Fiction (classic): 'Gulliver's Travels'

Pupil practice

Pupil Book pages 54–55

Get started

Ask children to write sentences to answer the questions, using quotations where possible.
Suggested answers:

1. When Gulliver woke up, he realised that he 'could not move' (and that 'the sun had just begun to rise above the horizon'). [1 mark]
2. Gulliver says that the little people were 'not much bigger than my middle finger'. [1 mark]
3. Gulliver reports that he was 'so astonished' when he first saw the little people that he 'roared aloud'. [1 mark]
4. After the little people returned, Gulliver reports, 'one climbed up to where he could get a full sight of my face' and called out '*Hekinah Degul!*' [1 mark]
5. Gulliver broke the strings that bound his left hand 'with a violent pull'. [1 mark]
6. After the little people had fired arrows at him, Gulliver decided 'not to anger my tiny captors further' and 'to think about how to get free later, when they had all gone away and left me alone'. [1 mark]
7. When Gulliver was hungry, he says, 'I put my finger to my mouth to indicate this'. [1 mark]
8. Gulliver thinks he might be in a place called 'Lilliput' because 'one little man, who seemed to be important' said it 'several times' in his 'long speech'. [1 mark]

Try these

Ask children to write sentences to answer the questions, explaining their answers as fully as they can. The children's answers may be subjective but should be in their own words and well justified, using evidence from either the text or the children's own experiences. **Possible answers:**

1. Answers should refer to what Gulliver calls 'a great crowd'. [1 mark]
2. Answers could suggest that the little people were afraid of Gulliver and/or the damage he could do. They could also, possibly with less justification, suggest that the little people intended to attack Gulliver. [2 marks]
3. As above, answers should refer to the little people's desire to protect themselves. They could also speculate that the people wanted to move/manipulate Gulliver and needed him to stay asleep. [2 marks]
4. Answers could refer to Gulliver's attempt 'to catch some of the annoying little creatures', but there is otherwise no evidence that he means to hurt them: he plans to attempt to escape only when 'they had all gone away and left me alone'. (He does seem to be able to free himself, with effort, so seems not to want to alarm them.) [2 marks]
5. Answers could refer to the little people building a tower, the 'important' little man giving a speech (presumably about Gulliver), the inhabitants feeding him a lot of 'deliciously cooked' food and/or to their doctors giving him a sleeping potion. They could suggest that this treatment is relatively friendly and that the little people did not really want to hurt Gulliver; they could alternatively suggest that the speech and sleeping potion suggest the little people have unknown and suspicious plans for him. [2 marks]
6. Answers should grasp that Gulliver is unable to see and is therefore unable to describe much of the setting, as his head is pinned to the ground. They could also suggest that the author wants the reader to concentrate on characters and action instead. [2 marks]
7. Gulliver refers to the little people as 'small creatures'; 'a tiny human creature not much bigger than my middle finger'; 'annoying little creatures'; 'tiny captors'; 'tiny people'; 'one little man'; 'quite friendly'; and 'inhabitants'. Answers could suggest that Gulliver stresses the size of the little people with almost every reference, but also that he changes from calling them 'creatures' to 'people' and 'inhabitants', and that this may suggest he has begun to see them as people and individuals rather than 'creatures'. [2 marks]
8. Answers could suggest that the phrase reveals that, later, Gulliver learns to communicate with and learn things from the little people. [2 marks]

Now try these

The children's answers will be subjective, but should be well justified where appropriate. **Possible answers:**

1. Answers could refer to Gulliver's initial astonishment, knowledge of several languages, understandable irritability, acceptance of his situation and reluctance to fight the little people or make them angry, appreciation of the tiny food and/or apparent interest in his bizarre surroundings. [3 marks max]
2. Phrases could include any of the following details: 'I tried to stand up but found to my astonishment that I could not move. My hands and feet and even my hair seemed to be fastened to the ground. The sun was getting hotter. Then I was horrified to feel some small creatures moving along my left leg and up to my chest'; 'I felt my left hand and my face pierced with hundreds of tiny arrows'; 'I heard some knocking near my right ear and the sound of a great crowd'; 'one little man […] made a long

Unit 13: Fiction (classic): 'Gulliver's Travels'

speech, not a word of which I could understand. He said the word 'Lilliput' several times'; 'They were deliciously cooked'; 'someone called out, *"Peplum selam"*'; 'At this, they loosened the cords that bound me a little'. Answers should recognise the senses described (touch, sound and taste).
[3 marks max]

3. Open-ended question: The little people say: *'Hekinah degul!'* when they first meet Gulliver (answers could suggest 'Greetings Giant!' / 'The giant's awake!' or similar); *'Tolgo phonac!'* just before the tiny archers fire arrows at Gulliver (answers could suggest 'Fire away!' or similar); and *'Peplum selam!'* just before the little people loosen Gulliver's cords (answers could suggest 'Loosen the cords' or similar). [3 marks max]

4. Open-ended question: Answers should grasp that the opening paragraph describes Gulliver's experience as he understands it, adding a small amount of information at a time and detailing the feelings he has before he can see their explanations. [3 marks max]

5. Open-ended question: Look for relevance to the topic, characters and situation, and the important little man's possible plans for Gulliver. The speech should use appropriately formal language.
[3 marks max]

Support, embed & challenge

Support
Use Unit 13 Resource 1: Gulliver's comic strip to support children in exploring the plot of the story. Ask children to retell the story using a comic strip layout and style. Support them to think about how they will divide the story into the number of boxes given in the comic strip template, and how they will use the thought and speech bubbles. Support children to summarise each scene to retell the story using minimal words.

Embed
Ask the children to rewrite the extract from the perspective of one of the little people. Ask: 'How did you or one of your fellows discover this giant?', 'Why did you tie him down?', 'How did you try to communicate with him?'

Challenge
Use Unit 13 Resource 2: A strange language to prompt the children to consider how the author may have invented the language of Lilliput. Once they have invented new words for those given on the worksheet, encourage the children to add more vocabulary. Ask: 'Can you use your new language to communicate with a partner?'

Homework / Additional activities

Travelling onwards
Ask children to find out more about *Gulliver's Travels* – by reading more of the book, watching a filmed adaptation or researching the story and its background on the internet. Ask children to be prepared to share their findings with the class or a group.

Collins Connect: Unit 13
Ask the children to complete Unit 13 (see Teach → Comprehension → Year 6 → Unit 13).

Unit 14: Playscript: 'Compere Lapin and Compere Tig'

Overview

English curriculum objectives

- Continue to read and discuss an increasingly wide range of fiction, poetry, plays, non-fiction and reference books or textbooks
- Increase their familiarity with a wide range of books, including myths, legends and traditional stories, modern fiction, fiction from our literary heritage, and books from other cultures and traditions
- Identify and discuss themes and conventions in and across a wide range of writing
- Prepare poems and plays to read aloud and to perform, showing understanding through intonation, tone and volume so that the meaning is clear to an audience
- Check that the book makes sense to them, discussing their understanding and exploring the meaning of words in context
- Ask questions to improve their understanding
- Draw inferences such as inferring characters' feelings, thoughts and motives from their actions, and justifying inferences with evidence
- Identify how language, structure and presentation contribute to meaning
- Discuss and evaluate how authors use language, including figurative language, considering the impact on the reader
- Participate in discussions about books that are read to them and those they can read for themselves, building on their own and others' ideas and challenging views courteously
- Explain and discuss their understanding of what they have read, including through formal presentations and debates, maintaining a focus on the topic and using notes where necessary
- Provide reasoned justification for their views

Treasure House resources

- Comprehension Skills Pupil Book 6, Unit 14, pages 56–59
- Collins Connect Treasure House Comprehension Year 6, Unit 14
- Photocopiable Unit 14, Resource 1: Finding the features, page 114
- Photocopiable Unit 14, Resource 2: A new trick, page 115

Additional resources

- Dictionaries or the internet (optional)

Introduction

Teaching overview

'Compere Lapin and Compere Tig' is a playscript version of one of many stories about Compere Lapin, a trickster character who originates in folk tales of the West Indies. Most of these stories involve animals like Lapin (a rabbit) and Tig (a tiger), as well as kings, queens and ordinary men, women and children. The text introduces children to the structure and presentation of a playscript as well as reminding them of the themes of folk tales and fables: stories originating in popular culture, typically passed on by word of mouth, typically with animals as characters and conveying a moral.

Introduce the text

Ask the children if they have heard of or know anything about the West Indies. If they have, invite them to share their knowledge with the class. Then ask what the children know about the form and conventions of playscripts, and briefly discuss the layout of the text.

Tell the children that in this lesson they will focus on a playscript of a West Indian folk tale. Then they will answer questions about the text. Remind children that sometimes the answers to the questions will be clearly written in the playscript, but that sometimes they may need to think a little harder and use their own ideas, supported by the text.

Ask the children to read the playscript individually or in pairs. Ask them to note down any words they do not understand. Discuss unknown or unusual vocabulary before setting children to work answering the questions in the Pupil Book. Try to avoid discussing the content of the text until after the children have answered the Pupil Book questions.

Unit 14: Playscript: 'Compere Lapin and Compere Tig'

Pupil practice

Pupil Book pages 58–59

Get started

Ask children to write sentences to answer the questions, using quotations where possible.
Suggested answers:

1. The setting for the scene is 'a lush green landscape with trees and a clear pool of water on a warm day'. [1 mark]
2. The characters in the scene are 'a King', 'Compere Lapin', 'Compere Tig', 'the King's guards' and 'a wise man'. [1 mark]
3. The King knows someone has been in his pool because 'the water is murky and dirty'. [1 mark]
4. The actor playing the King should be 'thundering' when he says 'He must die!' [1 mark]
5. The wise man tells the King, 'Compere Lapin is to blame'. [1 mark]
6. Compere Tig feels proud when he thinks he is allowed to bathe in the pool (he acts 'with pride' and says: 'What an honour.'). [1 mark]
7. When they capture Compere Tig, the guards 'wrap him in a bundle and tie him to a tree'. [1 mark]
8. Compere Tig lies to Compere Lapin when he tells him, 'the King is going to kill me because I refused to marry his daughter. It has nothing to do with the pool of clear water'. [1 mark]

Try these

Ask children to write sentences to answer the questions, explaining their answers as fully as they can. The children's answers may be subjective but should be in their own words and well justified, using evidence from either the text or the children's own experiences. **Possible answers:**

1. Answers should recognise that Lapin knows he 'dirtied the waters' of the King's pool and must have heard the King say, 'No-one visits my pool and lives'. [1 mark]
2. Answers should recognise that Lapin tells Tig that the King has given him permission to use the pool so Tig will be caught and punished for dirtying the pool in his place. [1 mark]
3. Answers should recognise that Tig has successfully tricked Lapin into believing that whoever is in the trap will be able to marry the King's daughter. [1 mark]
4. Answers should recognise that Tig and Lapin are fond of tricking one another, and could expand that the consequences of their tricks could result in death or serious injury; it is therefore likely that they feel strongly against one another. They could further suggest that Lapin appears to have started this antagonism by blaming Tig for dirtying the King's pool. [2 marks]

5. Open-ended question: Answers could suggest that Tig was justified as Lapin had tricked him first, or that tricking Lapin made Tig just as bad a character. [2 marks]
6. Answers could refer to the stage directions 'Compere Tig walks proudly to the pool and dips his paws in' and 'Compere Lapin sits washing his ears'. [2 marks]
7. Open-ended question: Answers should approximate Tig gloating, jeering or laughing cruelly in Lapin's direction. [2 marks]
8. Answers could suggest that the guards remaining onstage with the glowing iron bar acts as a reminder of the fate awaiting whichever Compere ends up in the bundle. [2 marks]

Now try these

The children's answers will be subjective, but should be well justified where appropriate. **Possible answers:**

1. Answers could refer to Lapin's sneaky use of the King's pool, panic at the prospect of being caught, deceptive nature, eagerness to marry the King's daughter and/or foolishness at being tricked by Tig. [3 marks max]
2. Answers could refer to the playscript's inclusion of the setting, character list, scene heading, stage directions, character line prompts and/ or direct speech written without speech marks. [3 marks max]
3. Open-ended question: Look for accurate definitions of the technical or more difficult terms in the playscript, including 'upstage', 'downstage', 'stage right' and 'stage left'. The words should be presented alphabetically. [3 marks max]
4. Open-ended question: Look for relevance to task, imagination, presentation and appropriateness of content to the setting, characters and the reality of a stage. Answers should acknowledge it would not be possible to have a pool or red hot iron on stage, for example, or to string someone up from a real tree. [3 marks max]
5. Open-ended question: Look for passages that contain all of the information from the text as a narrative that doesn't retain any features of a playscript. [3 marks max]

Unit 14: Playscript: 'Compere Lapin and Compere Tig'

Support, embed & challenge

Support
Use Unit 14 Resource 1: Finding the features to support children in familiarising themselves with the features of a playscript. Children should label the features with the terms supplied. They could also use coloured pens and highlighters to help with the identifications.

Embed
Use Unit 14 Resource 2: A new trick to assist children in planning a new, similar story for the trickster character of Compere Lapin. The children come up with a new trick he could try, and then structure a story around it.

Challenge
Ask the children to write the next scene of the playscript. They could improvise it in groups first. Encourage the children to think carefully about how the characters would act, asking: 'Can Compere Lapin get out of being burned by the King's guards?', 'Might he and Compare Tig start to work together, or will they keep tricking one another?' Remind children to include the features of playscripts such as stage directions and who says what.

Homework / Additional activities

Script spotting
Ask children to find other playscripts and to look at their features closely. Ask them to study what things are similar to and what are different from the features in the text. Ask them to be prepared to share their findings with the class or a group.

Collins Connect: Unit 14
Ask the children to complete Unit 14 (see Teach → Comprehension → Year 6 → Unit 14).

Review unit 2: Non-fiction (autobiography): 'Swimming the Dream'

Pupil Book pages 60–62

Get started

Ask children to write sentences to answer the questions, using quotations where possible.

Suggested answers:

1. Ellie had four siblings: 'I'm the youngest of five. I have three older sisters and one older brother'. [1 mark]

2. Ellie writes, 'I was born in 1994'. [1 mark]

3. Ellie 'grew up in Sutton Coldfield, in Birmingham, in a large road called Wood Lane'. [1 mark]

4. Ellie writes, 'I remember the house really well because of the swimming pool in the back garden, which had a wave machine and was brilliant fun. [1 mark]

5. Ellie moved from her first school because she 'didn't like it much': the 'lessons all went a bit too fast' and she 'found it really hard to keep up'. [2 marks]

6. Ellie's favourite subjects at school were 'P.E. and Art'. [1 mark]

7. Ellie next moved 'to Aldridge'. [1 mark]

8. Ellie describes her new house as 'a really nice, old house in a large cul-de-sac'. [1 mark]

Try these

Ask children to write sentences to answer the questions, explaining their answers as fully as they can. The children's answers may be subjective but should be in their own words and well justified, using evidence from either the text or the children's own experiences.

Possible answers:

1. Answers should recognise that the extract is an account of the author's own life, written in the first person and presented in chronological order. [2 marks]

2. Answers should grasp that an autobiography is written by the subject of the text (in the first person), whereas a biography is written by a different author, (usually in the third person). [2 marks]

3. Answers should recognise that Ellie writes that swimming suits her 'because it's a time-consuming sport and I like being busy' and could also mention the fact that it's a sociable sport. [2 marks]

4. Answers could mention numerous attractions of swimming, but they should recognise that Ellie states her initial reason for wanting to learn to swim was 'so that I could swim in our pool with everyone else'. [1 mark]

5. Open-ended question: Look for well-reasoned opinions. Answers may refer to Ellie having a swimming pool at her first house, having siblings that she wanted to emulate by being able to swim, her preference for sporty activities and the fact that her parents allowed her to take swimming lessons from the age of five. [2 marks]

6. Answers should recognise the style of the extract as being direct and relatively informal. They could give examples that include first-person narration, short sentences, use of contractions, use of dashes and exclamation marks, use of informal language ('on the go'; 'I didn't do sitting quietly'; 'I didn't like it much') and conversational tone (for example, 'So, …'; 'I can never decide …').

7. Answers should grasp that the dash indicates a pause that both separates and connects the two parts of the sentence. The part of the sentence that comes after the dash provides an explanation for the assertion made before it. [2 marks]

8. Open-ended question: Answers are most likely to give a positive answer, although Ellie didn't enjoy the academic subjects at school and initially found leaving her friends 'upsetting'. Evidence for a positive answer could include the facts that she had 'brilliant fun' at the house with the swimming pool and wave machine, she had friends across the road, she was always 'on the go' and playing 'outdoors', she was able to start swimming lessons at an early age, and she was able to leave a school she didn't like. [2 marks]

Review unit 2: Non-fiction (autobiography): 'Swimming the Dream'

Now try these

The children's answers will be subjective, but should be well justified where appropriate.

Possible answers:

1. Answers could refer to Ellie's love of fun and activity, friendliness, love of the outdoors, preference for being 'on the go' / 'active' / 'on the move' / 'busy', determination, creativity, aversion to academic subjects and outgoing nature. [2 marks]

2. Open-ended question: Look for relevant questions directed at Ellie that are not answered by the extract, for example: *How often did you go swimming? When did you enter your first swimming competition? Did you have any time for other hobbies?* [3 marks max]

3. Open-ended question: Look for relevance to task, imagination, presentation and inclusion of details about Ellie's childhood from the text (such as where she lived, her favourite school subjects and her hobbies). [3 marks max]

4. Open-ended question: Answers should consider the main facts required to write an autobiography and follow on from the 'Swimming from the start' section in the extract. They could mention achievements, plans, feelings and any life-changing events. [3 marks max]

5. Open-ended question: Look for relevance to task, imagination, presentation and inclusion of details about Ellie's childhood from the text. [3 marks max]

Unit 15: Non-fiction (autobiography): 'Wild Swans'

Overview

English curriculum objectives

- Continue to read and discuss an increasingly wide range of fiction, poetry, plays, non-fiction and reference books or textbooks
- Read books that are structured in different ways and read for a range of purposes
- Identify and discuss themes and conventions in and across a wide range of writing
- Check that the book makes sense to them, discussing their understanding and exploring the meaning of words in context
- Ask questions to improve their understanding
- Summarise the main ideas drawn from more than one paragraph, identifying key details that support the main idea
- Identify how language, structure and presentation contribute to meaning
- Distinguish between statements of fact and opinion
- Retrieve, record and present information from non-fiction
- Participate in discussions about books that are read to them and those they can read for themselves, building on their own and others' ideas and challenging views courteously
- Explain and discuss their understanding of what they have read, including through formal presentations and debates, maintaining a focus on the topic and using notes where necessary
- Provide reasoned justification for their views

Treasure House resources

- Comprehension Skills Pupil Book 6, Unit 15, pages 63–66
- Collins Connect Treasure House Comprehension Year 6, Unit 15
- Photocopiable Unit 15, Resource 1: Questions about China, page 116
- Photocopiable Unit 15, Resource 2: Researching China, page 117

Additional resources

- Dictionaries or the internet (optional)
- *Wild Swans* by Jung Chang, whole text (optional)

Introduction

Teaching overview

Wild Swans is an autobiographical extract by Jung Chang. In the extract, Jung Chang remembers being six years old and living in a regime under Chairman Mao, who had ordered the people of China to assist in the production of vast quantities of steel. The text provides children with the opportunity to explore an autobiographical text written in chronological order.

Introduce the extract

Ask the children if they know anything about China. If they do, invite them to share their knowledge with the class. Then ask what the children know about the form and conventions of autobiographies.

Tell the children that in this lesson they will focus on one extract from an autobiography by a woman called Jung Chang. Then they will answer questions about the extract. Remind children that sometimes the answers to the questions will be clearly written in the extract, but that sometimes they may need to think a little harder and use their own ideas, supported by the text.

Ask the children to read the extract individually or in pairs. Ask them to note down any words they do not understand. Discuss unknown or unusual vocabulary before setting children to work answering the questions in the Pupil Book. Try to avoid discussing the content of the extract until after the children have answered the Pupil Book questions.

Unit 15: Non-fiction (autobiography): 'Wild Swans'

Pupil practice

Pupil Book pages 65–66

Get started

Ask children to write sentences to answer the questions, using quotations where possible. **Suggested answers:**

1. The text says that 'Jung Chang was born in Yibin, Sichuan Province in China'. [1 mark]
2. The text says that she wrote 'Wild Swans' 'partly as her autobiography and partly as a biography describing the lives of her mother and grandmother'. [1 mark]
3. Jung Chang was six when she started primary school. [1 mark]
4. On her journeys to and from school, she searched 'for broken nails, rusty cogs, and any other metal objects that had been trodden into the mud between the cobbles'. [1 mark]
5. She needed them 'for feeding into furnaces to produce steel'. [1 mark]
6. The slogans on the walls said, 'Long Live the Great Leap Forward!' and 'Everybody, Make Steel!' [1 mark]
7. Chairman Mao was the leader of China. [1 mark]
8. The cooking woks were replaced by 'crucible-like vats'. [1 mark]

Try these

Ask children to write sentences to answer the questions, explaining their answers as fully as they can. The children's answers may be subjective but should be in their own words and well justified, using evidence from either the text or the children's own experiences. **Possible answers:**

1. Answers should appreciate that an autobiography is an account of the author's own life. [1 mark]
2. Answers could refer to features such as factual information presented in chronological order and in the first person. The information covers Chang's childhood, its circumstances and their impact. [2 marks]
3. Answers should recognise this sentence assumes that the reader is surprised by the previous piece of information (that the metal objects she collected 'were for feeding into furnaces to produce steel, which was my major occupation'). They could add that it answers an assumed question such as 'Did you really have a major occupation at the age of six?' and creates the impression that the author is speaking with the reader rather than just informing them. [2 marks]
4. Answers should grasp that Mao's main aim for China was that it should produce huge amounts of steel. [1 mark]
5. Answers could refer to education, health, healthcare, home life, nutrition and/or agriculture. [2 marks]
6. Answers should grasp that Jung Chang did not agree with Mao's plan, and could refer to her calling it a 'half-baked dream'. [2 marks]
7. Answers should recognise that Jung Chang mentions an alternative when she says: 'But instead of trying to expand the proper steel industry with skilled workers, he decided to get the whole population to take part.' [1 mark]
8. Open-ended question: Look for well-reasoned opinions (although it is less likely that children will be able to justify an affirmative answer). [2 marks]

Now try these

The children's answers will be subjective, but should be well justified where appropriate. **Possible answers:**

1. In addition to worrying about her daughter, answers could refer to Chang's mother having to move out of her home ('the old vicarage') and into a compound, having to stop cooking for her family, having to give up her woks and soft, comfortable bed and/or her and her husband having to stay in their offices, away from each other and their daughter, 'to make sure the temperature in their office furnaces never dropped'. [3 marks max]
2. Open-ended question: Look for relevant questions directed at Jung Chang that are not answered by the extract, for example: *How did you feel about leaving your home and not seeing your parents often? How did you learn to read and write well, without any lessons at school? Did you have any time to make friends?* [3 marks max]
3. Open-ended question: Look for relevance to task, consistency of theme and character, imagination, presentation and consideration of things that Chang might like or not mind, as well as things that make her unhappy. [3 marks max]
4. Open-ended question: Look for relevance to task, imagination, presentation and inclusion of details about Chang's childhood from the text, for example: her 'main occupation', her poor schooling, her life in the compound and her lack of contact with her parents. [3 marks max]
5. Answers should consider the main facts required to write an autobiography: date and place of birth, family life, childhood and schooling, hobbies, achievements, plans, feelings and any life-changing events. [3 marks max]

Unit 15: Non-fiction (autobiography): 'Wild Swans'

Support, embed & challenge

Support
Use Unit 15 Resource 1: Questions about China to support children in understanding how specific pieces of information can be found in information texts. The children read two short passages about China, and then compose three questions about each. Ask pairs to swap questions and answer each other's, to check that the questions are relevant to the passages.

Embed
Use Unit 15 Resource 2: Researching China to encourage children to conduct further research about China. Help children to plan their questions, if required. For example, ask: 'Where is China?', 'How big is it?', 'What wildlife is there?', 'What are people's homes like?' Then ask children to research the answers to their questions and present their findings as either a fact file or a presentation that can be shared with others.

Challenge
Ask the children to use their notes to write an autobiography of their own life so far. Remind them to use the correct order, and to think carefully about how they could link their earliest and/or most important memories to who they are now.

Homework / Additional activities

Autobiography authors
Ask the children to research autobiographies, and to find five people who have written them. They should note down who each person is and what interesting things they have done. Ask children to be prepared to share their findings with the class or a group.

Collins Connect: Unit 15
Ask the children to complete Unit 15 (see Teach → Comprehension → Year 6 → Unit 15).

Unit 16: Poetry: 'Rebecca (Who Slammed Doors for Fun and Perished Miserably)'

Overview

English curriculum objectives

- Continue to read and discuss an increasingly wide range of fiction, poetry, plays, non-fiction and reference books or textbooks
- Identify and discuss themes and conventions in and across a wide range of writing
- Learn a wider range of poetry by heart
- Prepare poems and plays to read aloud and to perform, showing understanding through intonation, tone and volume so that the meaning is clear to an audience
- Check that the book makes sense to them, discussing their understanding and exploring the meaning of words in context
- Ask questions to improve their understanding
- Draw inferences such as inferring characters' feelings, thoughts and motives from their actions, and justifying inferences with evidence
- Identify how language, structure and presentation contribute to meaning
- Discuss and evaluate how authors use language, including figurative language, considering the impact on the reader
- Participate in discussions about books that are read to them and those they can read for themselves, building on their own and others' ideas and challenging views courteously
- Explain and discuss their understanding of what they have read, including through formal presentations and debates, maintaining a focus on the topic and using notes where necessary
- Provide reasoned justification for their views

Treasure House resources

- Comprehension Skills Pupil Book 6, Unit 16, pages 67–69
- Photocopiable Unit 16, Resource 1: Poem pieces, page 118
- Photocopiable Unit 16, Resource 2: Poem planner, page 119

Additional resources

- Dictionaries or the internet (optional)
- *Cautionary Tales for Children* by Hilaire Belloc, whole text (optional)

Introduction

Teaching overview

'Rebecca (Who Slammed Doors for Fun and Perished Miserably)' is a simple narrative poem that tells the story of a young girl with an annoying habit – and her sticky end. It is a funny, farcical tale with a straightforward message: don't slam doors. It was published in 1907 as part of the Anglo-French writer Hilaire Belloc's book of similar amusing and grisly verses, *Cautionary Tales for Children*.

Introduce the poem

Ask the children if any of them have heard of the poet Hilaire Belloc. If they have, invite them to share their knowledge with the class. If possible, share one or two of his other poems so children get a feel for his style of writing.

Tell the children that in this lesson they will focus on one poem. Then they will answer questions about it. Remind children that sometimes the answers to the questions will be clearly written in the poem, but that sometimes they may need to think a little harder and use their own ideas, supported by the text.

Ask the children to read the poem individually or in pairs. Ask them to note down any words they do not understand. Discuss unknown or unusual vocabulary before setting children to work answering the questions in the Pupil Book. Try to avoid discussing the content of the poem until after the children have answered the Pupil Book questions.

Unit 16: Poetry: 'Rebecca (Who Slammed Doors for Fun and Perished Miserably)'

Pupil practice

Pupil Book pages 68–69

Get started

Ask children to write sentences to answer the questions, using quotations where possible.
Suggested answers:

1. 'Abhors' means to hate something and treat it with disgust; in this example, people hate the trick of little girls slamming doors. [1 mark]
2. Rebecca's full name is 'Rebecca Offendort'. [1 mark]
3. Rebecca's father is 'a wealthy banker'. [1 mark]
4. Rebecca 'lived in Palace Green, Bayswater'. [1 mark]
5. Rebecca annoyed others by 'slamming doors'. (She was 'given to this furious sport.') [1 mark]
6. She would 'make her Uncle Jacob start' (that is, she startled him / made him jump). [1 mark]
7. A 'marble bust / Of Abraham' fell on her from above the door. [1 mark]
8. Several 'children' from 'far and near' were 'brought to hear / The awful tale' at Rebecca's funeral. [1 mark]

Try these

Ask children to write sentences to answer the questions, explaining their answers as fully as they can. The children's answers may be subjective but should be in their own words and well justified, using evidence from either the text or the children's own experiences. **Possible answers:**

1. Answers could mention Rebecca being 'given to this furious sport' of slamming doors 'deliberately', her disregard of (or pleasure in) making 'her Uncle Jacob start', her being 'not really bad at heart, / But only rather rude and wild', her being 'an aggravating child' and to the speaker's description of her (perhaps sarcastically) as a 'little lamb'. [2 marks]
2. Answers could suggest that Rebecca liked slamming doors because she thought it was fun to startle people / her Uncle Jacob specifically, or that she simply enjoyed it and was too 'rude and wild' to worry about the consequences of her actions. They could also infer that slamming doors may have been a way for Rebecca to gain attention, perhaps from her 'wealthy banker' father. [2 marks]
3. The reactions of Rebecca's parents are not described in the poem, but answers should show some reasoned judgement. They could suggest that her parents were too busy to notice or care, noting that Rebecca's father is a described as a 'wealthy banker' (although Rebecca's mother isn't mentioned at all). Alternatively, they may suggest that her parents were not happy about her behaviour, based on perceptions of how their own parents would react. [2 marks]
4. Answers should detect that the person giving the funeral sermon seems to disapprove of Rebecca's behaviour, as he/she appears to have used the sermon to teach the attending children a lesson. The sermon 'Mentioned her virtues, it is true, / But dwelt upon her vices too, / And showed the dreadful end of one / Who goes and slams the door for fun.' We also know it was 'long' and constituted an 'awful tale' that 'much impressed' its listeners. [2 marks]
5. Answers should appreciate that the children who heard the story of what happened to Rebecca 'inly swore / They never more would slam the door / – As often they had done before.' The story may have warned them, therefore, and caused them to promise to behave, but the last line implies that this is a promise that has been broken before and so therefore may be broken again. [2 marks]
6. Answers should recognise that the final lines of the poem, 'They never more would slam the door / – As often they had done before' indicate that other children also like to slam doors. [1 mark]
7. Answers could refer to the warning given by the poem, and conclude that it does discourage children from slamming doors by showing them the dire consequences. Alternatively, they could refer to the humour of the poem and suggest that it encourages (or, at least, does not discourage) children in the slamming of doors because the consequences described are far-fetched and unrealistic – and, perhaps, that the humour of the poem reflects the mischievous fun of the activity itself. [2 marks]
8. Answers could take the content of the poem at face value, and suggest that slamming doors can really be dangerous as it can startle and/or hurt people (including those doing it). They are perhaps more likely to conclude that there is no real danger described in the poem (as the consequences described are far-fetched and unrealistic), and could suggest that the true purpose of the poem is to entertain and/or poke fun at the kinds of people who exaggerate the consequences of actions they dislike. [2 marks]

Now try these

The children's answers will be subjective, but should be well justified where appropriate. **Possible answers:**

1. 'Virtues' could include enthusiasm, sense of humour and her being 'not really bad at heart'. 'Vices' could include her treatment of Uncle Jacob, her being 'rude and wild', her being 'aggravating' and, of course, her bad habit of slamming doors. [4 marks max]

Unit 16: Poetry: 'Rebecca (Who Slammed Doors for Fun and Perished Miserably)'

2. Answers should suggest that the information in brackets adds to the story by providing extra details, and could add that the text upholds the rhythmic structure of the lines in the poem. They should also state that brackets are used because the extra information is not strictly necessary to the tale, and could add that they break up the flow of the verse with a comment, which makes the speaker's tone appear conversational. [2 marks]

3. Answers should explain that the poem is organised into rhyming couplets. The rhyming couplets add to the flow and rhythm of the poem, which in turn add to the humour and narrative style.
[3 marks max]

4. Open-ended question: Look for relevance to task, consistency of character and theme, imagination and presentation. [3 marks max]

5. Answers should detect that this is a humorous poem. The humour is created by the unrealistic and farcical content, and exaggeration of the effects of Rebecca's behaviour. It is also aided by the speaker's sardonic tone ('it happened that a marble bust'; 'little lamb') and regular switches between formal, stuffy or disapproving language ('abhors'; 'aggravating child') and more informal, childlike glee ('slam the door like billy-o'; 'It knocked her flat!'). The humour is also emphasised by the poem's bouncing rhythm and rhyming couplets. [3 marks max]

Support, embed & challenge

Support
Use Unit 16 Resource 1: Poem pieces to support children in exploring the composition of the poem by replacing some of its key elements with ideas of their own. If children find they can achieve this task, they could then continue their new version of the poem using the text for guidance.

Embed
Use Unit 16 Resource 2: Poem planner to encourage children to write a humorous, apparently moral poem of their own devising, using a structure of their own. Ask them to use the planning sheet to structure their ideas and then to begin their poems.

Challenge
Ask children to research other poems by Hilaire Belloc, and some information about the poet himself. Ask them to be prepared to share their findings with the class or a group, and to prepare a reading of the poem(s) they find.

Homework / Additional activities

When you were young…
Ask children to ask their parents, carers and/or other adults what stories their relatives and teachers told them to put them off behaving badly when they were young. Ask: 'Were there any stories as far-fetched as the one in Rebecca?', 'Would any of the stories make amusing poems or tales?'.

Unit 17: Fiction (modern): 'Project Bright Spark'

Overview

English curriculum objectives

- Continue to read and discuss an increasingly wide range of fiction, poetry, plays, non-fiction and reference books or textbooks
- Increase their familiarity with a wide range of books, including myths, legends and traditional stories, modern fiction, fiction from our literary heritage, and books from other cultures and traditions
- Recommend books that they have read to their peers, giving reasons for their choices
- Identify and discuss themes and conventions in and across a wide range of writing
- Make comparisons within and across books
- Check that the book makes sense to them, discussing their understanding and exploring the meaning of words in context
- Ask questions to improve their understanding
- Draw inferences such as inferring characters' feelings, thoughts and motives from their actions, and justifying inferences with evidence
- Predict what might happen from details stated and implied
- Identify how language, structure and presentation contribute to meaning
- Discuss and evaluate how authors use language, including figurative language, considering the impact on the reader
- Participate in discussions about books that are read to them and those they can read for themselves, building on their own and others' ideas and challenging views courteously
- Explain and discuss their understanding of what they have read, including through formal presentations and debates, maintaining a focus on the topic and using notes where necessary
- Provide reasoned justification for their views

Treasure House resources

- Comprehension Skills Pupil Book 6, Unit 17, pages 70–72
- Photocopiable Unit 17, Resource 1: Briony's character, page 120
- Photocopiable Unit 17, Resource 2: Bright Spark storyboard, page 121

Additional resources

- Dictionaries or the internet (optional)
- *Project Bright Spark* by Annabel Pitcher, whole text (optional)

Introduction

Teaching overview

Project Bright Spark is a story about a girl called Briony and her discovery of a conspiracy involving her teacher. It encourages children to draw inferences regarding characters' feelings, thoughts and motives from their actions, and to justify inferences with evidence. There are opportunities to develop children's ability to evaluate how authors use language to portray characters' feelings, thoughts and motives, considering the impact on the reader.

Introduce the extract

Ask the children if any of them know any stories about child detectives or science fiction mysteries. If they do, invite them to share their knowledge with the class.

Tell the children that in this lesson they will focus on one extract from a story called *Project Bright Spark*. Then they will answer questions about the extract. Remind children that sometimes the answers to the questions will be clearly written in the extract, but that sometimes they may need to think a little harder and use their own ideas, supported by the text.

Ask the children to read the extract individually or in pairs. Ask them to note down any words they do not understand. Discuss unknown or unusual vocabulary before setting children to work answering the questions in the Pupil Book. Try to avoid discussing the content of the extract until after the children have answered the Pupil Book questions.

Unit 17: Fiction (modern): 'Project Bright Spark'

Pupil practice

Pupil Book pages 71–72

Get started

Ask children to write sentences to answer the questions, using quotations where possible.
Suggested answers:

1. The speaker was hiding in 'the cupboard'. [1 mark]
2. The extract says, 'Mildred had stolen the school trip money'. [1 mark]
3. The extract says, 'Mr Crabtree had called up the school, pretending to be a headteacher.' [1 mark]
4. The speaker's skin went cold because she saw that, next to her 'own name' 'were the sinister words: *teach her a lesson*'. [1 mark]
5. The extract says, 'A clock ticked slowly.' [1 mark]
6. The speaker thought she could hear 'the other children putting on their coats downstairs'. This would mean that 'the party had finished', and her parents would 'be so worried' as she was missing. [2 marks]
7. When the speaker sat down and rested her head against the wood, she felt 'anxious'. [1 mark]
8. The large, dark shape looming in the shadows was 'Mr Spark'. [1 mark]

Try these

Ask children to write sentences to answer the questions, explaining their answers as fully as they can. The children's answers may be subjective but should be in their own words and well justified, using evidence from either the text or the children's own experiences. **Possible answers:**

1. Answers could detect that the speaker needed to hold the blue folder up to the keyhole to be able to see what it said, as it was dark in the cupboard and the keyhole was letting in some light. [2 marks]
2. Answers should mention that the speaker thought Mr Crabtree hadn't noticed anything suspicious because of the 'way he was working', and that this likely means he had continued to work uninterrupted. [2 marks]
3. Answers should recognise that Miss Cartwright and Mr Spark are the speaker's teachers. Aside from her using formal names from them, this information should be inferred from mentions of 'the school trip money', 'the school' the recommendation from 'a headteacher' and Mr Spark putting someone 'to the top of the class'. [2 marks]
4. Answers should state that one page in the blue folder had confused the speaker because it contained a 'labelled diagram of Mr Spark' with ' lots of technical stuff that didn't make any sense because it talked about wires and batteries and electrical parts'. The implication is that it is unusual to have a labelled technical diagram of a person. [2 marks]
5. When Mildred stole the school trip money, she planned to put it 'in Miss Cartwright's purse to get her sacked'. We also know that her replacement, Mr Spark, received 'instructions to put Mildred to the top of the class'. Answers should conclude that Mildred's ultimate goal was to reach the top of the class. [1 mark]
6. Answers should suggest that the speaker hadn't noticed the curtain or the depth of the cupboard earlier as she was so worried about being seen by Mr Crabtree, she was interested in the contents of the blue folder and/or listening so intently to the sounds from downstairs and considering her parents. [2 marks]
7. Answers should detect that the speaker scrambled silently to her knees because she was trying to get a better view of the dark shape in the shadows (she also says she 'leant forward, screwing up my eyes'), and/or because she felt a 'prickle of fear' and so was on high alert and wanted to be able to move more quickly. [2 marks]
8. Answers should explain that the speaker finally realised that Mr Spark was not human. Answers may further speculate that he was a robot, as the speaker reports 'a metallic sort of crash as a screw fell out of a joint in his neck', and reconsiders his 'lifeless eyes', 'swivelling neck' and 'weird behaviour'. [2 marks]

Now try these

The children's answers will be subjective, but should be well justified where appropriate. **Possible answers:**

1. Answers could refer to the speaker's daring and inquisitive nature, intelligence in working out the conspiracy and self-control as she remains quiet in the cupboard. They may also describe the speaker's behaviour as foolish or risky. [2 marks]
2. Answers could refer to the speaker's fear of being caught, relief at hiding effectively, curiosity regarding the blue folder, surprise/shock at the information the folder contained, disgust at the plot's benefit for Mildred, fear in response to the words next to her name, confusion at the technical diagram, boredom as time dragged on, anxiety that the party was ending, curiosity about the curtain in the cupboard, nervousness and then fear as she investigates it, shock at seeing Mr Spark and astonished realisation that he isn't human. [3 marks max]
3. Answers should suggest that the examples of ellipsis represent the moments the speaker is taking in what she sees. They could add that this helps the reader to read that section with pauses

Unit 17: Fiction (modern): 'Project Bright Spark'

and creates a feeling of suspense and tension, creating a build up to the moment the speaker realises that the figure in the cupboard is Mr Spark. [3 marks max]

4. Open-ended question: Look for relevance to task, consistency of character and theme, imagination and presentation. [3 marks max]

5. Open-ended question: Look for relevance to task including appropriate email format, consistency of character and theme, imagination and presentation. [3 marks max]

Support, embed & challenge

Support
Use Unit 17 Resource 1: Briony's character to support children in exploring the character of the speaker, Briony, further. Children should reread the text carefully to extract information that they can use in the profile. If the information isn't easily located in the extract, discuss with the children what the answers could be, encouraging them to infer ideas from the text and expand their own thoughts about Briony.

Embed
Use Unit 17 Resource 2: Bright Spark storyboard to encourage children to consider the visual aspects of the story. Ask children to imagine they are directing a television adaptation of the extract, and that they have to plan how each shot will look. Ask: 'What camera positions will there be?', 'What things will you show and when?' The scene is silent, but ask them then to compose a voiceover of Briony's thoughts so the viewer can hear them. Ask: 'How would Briony express her thoughts?'

Challenge
Ask the children to rewrite the extract from the perspective of Mr Crabtree. If you feel children would benefit from a starting prompt, suggest that Mr Crabtree thinks he can hear something in the cupboard, but at first just assumes that Mr Spark (the robot) has been left turned on.

Homework / Additional activities

What happens next?
Ask children to write the next part of the story using information from the extract (the evidence the speaker has found; her position in the cupboard) and their imagination. Remind them that their extension should be in keeping with the speaker's personality and feelings.

Unit 18: Fiction: 'The 39 Steps'

Overview

English curriculum objectives

- Continue to read and discuss an increasingly wide range of fiction, poetry, plays, non-fiction and reference books or textbooks
- Increase their familiarity with a wide range of books, including myths, legends and traditional stories, modern fiction, fiction from our literary heritage, and books from other cultures and traditions
- Recommend books that they have read to their peers, giving reasons for their choices
- Identify and discuss themes and conventions in and across a wide range of writing
- Make comparisons within and across books
- Check that the book makes sense to them, discussing their understanding and exploring the meaning of words in context
- Ask questions to improve their understanding
- Draw inferences such as inferring characters' feelings, thoughts and motives from their actions, and justifying inferences with evidence
- Predict what might happen from details stated and implied
- Identify how language, structure and presentation contribute to meaning
- Discuss and evaluate how authors use language, including figurative language, considering the impact on the reader
- Participate in discussions about books that are read to them and those they can read for themselves, building on their own and others' ideas and challenging views courteously
- Explain and discuss their understanding of what they have read, including through formal presentations and debates, maintaining a focus on the topic and using notes where necessary
- Provide reasoned justification for their views

Treasure House resources

- Comprehension Skills Pupil Book 6, Unit 18, pages 73–75
- Photocopiable Unit 18, Resource 1: Making decisions, page 122
- Photocopiable Unit 18, Resource 2: Timeline, page 123

Additional resources

- Dictionaries or the internet (optional)
- *The 39 Steps* by Andrew Lane, whole text (optional)

Introduction

Teaching overview

The 39 Steps is an adventure story about the main character Richard Hannay's involvement in a plot filled with assassination attempts, threats of war, murder and spies. It encourages children to draw inferences regarding characters' feelings, thoughts and motives from their actions, and to justify inferences with evidence. There are opportunities to develop children's ability to evaluate how authors use language to portray characters' feelings, thoughts and motives, considering the impact on the reader.

Introduce the extract

Ask the children if any of them know the story *The 39 Steps* or any other spy tales. If they do, invite them to share their knowledge with the class.

Tell the children that in this lesson they will focus on one extract from the story. Then they will answer questions about the extract. Remind children that sometimes the answers to the questions will be clearly written in the extract, but that sometimes they may need to think a little harder and use their own ideas, supported by the text.

Ask the children to read the extract individually or in pairs. Ask them to note down any words they do not understand. Discuss unknown or unusual vocabulary before setting children to work answering the questions in the Pupil Book. Try to avoid discussing the content of the extract until after the children have answered the Pupil Book questions.

Unit 18: Fiction: 'The 39 Steps'

Pupil practice

Pupil Book pages 74–75

Get started

Ask children to write sentences to answer the questions, using quotations where possible.
Suggested answers:

1. In Dumfries, the speaker changed trains, 'exchanging the fast train for a slow, rickety one that stopped at every station'. [1 mark]
2. On the slow, rickety train the people were 'local people – mostly men in hairy jackets, with whiskers, either going to market or returning from one'. [1 mark]
3. The speaker was wearing a 'tweed suit' (and was 'unshaven'). [1 mark]
4. The speaker's plan was 'to walk to a station two or three stops up the line, and catch a train heading south', back the way he'd come. This was to try to evade the police. [1 mark]
5. The speaker thought that the police might think he was hiding 'in some cottage'. [1 mark]
6. The small station the speaker found was in a 'remote' location, 'sheltering in a valley'. [1 mark]
7. The speaker went to sleep 'in the heather'. [1 mark]
8. In the morning, the speaker heard 'the distant whistle of a train'. [1 mark]

Try these

Ask children to write sentences to answer the questions, explaining their answers as fully as they can. The children's answers may be subjective but should be in their own words and well justified, using evidence from either the text or the children's own experiences. **Possible answers:**

1. Answers should refer to the 'hills and glens, crisscrossed with wide stretches of moorland and sparkling blue lakes'. Although there is no description of the landscape before it changed, answers may infer that it was dissimilar from the description given – perhaps built up, residential, dull and/or grimy. [2 marks]
2. Answers should deduce that most of the talk was about the prices the men could get for their lambs or cows because they were going to or coming from the markets in the countryside through which they were passing, and therefore that the men were likely to be farmers who sell their livestock. [2 marks]
3. Answers should recognise that the speaker left the slow train when he did because the only people in his carriage who could have remembered him 'were asleep', and could therefore conclude that he was avoiding anyone witnessing where he got off. [2 marks]
4. Answers should suggest that the speaker didn't check the name of the station because it didn't matter to him: the exact location was not important, just that no one saw where he alighted. Answers could also suggest that the man was too busy thinking about the next part of his plan, or perhaps that he was too tired or anxious to care. [2 marks]
5. Answers should discern that the weather was still and 'cold, smelling of heather and peat', although not freezing (the man chose to sleep without looking for shelter and seems not to be wearing a coat), and that there were clear skies: 'the hills seemed diamond sharp against the deep blue sky'. [2 marks]
6. Answers should refer to 'the fact that Scudder's body would have been found by now' and infer that a dead body had been discovered and must somehow be thought to be linked to the speaker. [2 marks]
7. Clues that the speaker is not guilty could include the fact that, when describing his plans, he focuses on staying 'out of trouble' until he could work out 'who to tell about the plot against Mr Karolides'. This implies the situation is not a straightforward escape from justice. The speaker also makes no reference to being guilty, despite the fact that he is narrating his own story: for example, he says that he is 'probably wanted by the police', but not that the police would be hunting him for killing Scudder. Answers may also refer to the fact that the reader's sympathies seem to be with the speaker (perhaps asserting that he seems pleasant). [2 marks]
8. Open-ended question: Answers could speculate that the speaker wants to tell someone about the plot against Mr Karolides so something can be done to prevent the plot happening, or to exonerate himself from involvement in Scudder's murder. [2 marks]

Now try these

The children's answers will be subjective, but should be well justified where appropriate. **Possible answers:**

1. Answers could refer to the speaker's observant nature, relatively calm demeanour given that he is on the run from the police, rationality and intelligence (based on the logic of his plans) and bravery or determination with regards to attempting to stop the plot against Mr Karolides despite his situation. [3 marks max]
2. Answers could include reference to the speaker's fear of being caught, curiosity about the new places and people he sees, tiredness during his long journey, despair at his coldness and hunger, determination to stop the plot against Mr Karolides, relief at being able to find a place to

Unit 18: Fiction: 'The 39 Steps'

sleep and panic at waking in the morning to catch the train. [3 marks max]
3. Open-ended question: Look for relevance to task, consistency of character and theme, imagination and presentation. [3 marks max]
4. Answers may perceive that the use of a short sentence followed by a longer sentence echoes the suddenness of waking up with a start and then the speaker's gathering of his bearings to continue with his journey. [3 marks max]
5. Answers could include any three relevant words or phrases. Some focus solely on time: 'eventually', 'by now', 'for a long time', 'It was early evening', 'At last', 'It was morning'. Answers could also, however, refer to phrases that refer to the passage of the journey: 'at every station', 'as we travelled', 'for a few stations'. [3 marks max]

Support, embed & challenge

Support
Use Unit 18 Resource 1: Making decisions to support children in exploring further each decision the man makes. They should identify each decision taken, and then give a reason for it using either the text or their imagination. One example is given.

Embed
Use Unit 18 Resource 2: Timeline to encourage children to create a timeline of everything that they know has happened to the man in real-time order, using both the text and their imagination. They should start with the speaker's first encounter with Scudder (the dead man) and will involve them creating the man's back story. It could be expanded, if you wish, into a possible early chapter of the story.

Challenge
Ask the children to rewrite the extract from the perspective of a policeman trying to hunt down the speaker. Ask them to use the extract to guide their tale of the journey as the policeman makes it, and include the policeman's thoughts about what the suspect has done and where he could be.

Homework / Additional activities

What are the 39 steps?
Reveal that the big mystery in the story turns out to be finding out what 'the 39 steps' are. Tell the children that film directors adapting the story have often changed the answer, so the ending of the tale remains a mystery! Ask children to invent any story that explains what the phrase 'the 39 steps' might mean. Ask them to use the information in the extract as well as their imaginations.

Unit 19: Non-fiction (autobiography): 'Benjamin Zephaniah: My Story'

Overview

English curriculum objectives

- Continue to read and discuss an increasingly wide range of fiction, poetry, plays, non-fiction and reference books or textbooks
- Read books that are structured in different ways and read for a range of purposes
- Identify and discuss themes and conventions in and across a wide range of writing
- Check that the book makes sense to them, discussing their understanding and exploring the meaning of words in context
- Ask questions to improve their understanding
- Summarise the main ideas drawn from more than one paragraph, identifying key details that support the main idea
- Identify how language, structure and presentation contribute to meaning
- Distinguish between statements of fact and opinion
- Retrieve, record and present information from non-fiction
- Participate in discussions about books that are read to them and those they can read for themselves, building on their own and others' ideas and challenging views courteously
- Explain and discuss their understanding of what they have read, including through formal presentations and debates, maintaining a focus on the topic and using notes where necessary
- Provide reasoned justification for their views

Treasure House resources

- Comprehension Skills Pupil Book 6, Unit 19, pages 76–78
- Photocopiable Unit 19, Resource 1: Fact or opinion?, page 124
- Photocopiable Unit 19, Resource 2: Planning a lesson, page 125

Additional resources

- Dictionaries or the internet (optional)
- *Benjamin Zephaniah: My Story* by Benjamin Zephaniah, whole text (optional)

Introduction

Teaching overview

Benjamin Zephaniah: My Story is an autobiographical text by the poet, novelist and playwright Benjamin Zephaniah. In the extract, Benjamin tells the reader about his memories of early childhood: where he lived and what his family's life was like. The text provides children with the opportunity to explore an autobiographical text written in chronological order, with content children may be able to relate to.

Introduce the extract

Ask the children if any of them have heard of the poet Benjamin Zephaniah or know any of his poems. If they have, invite them to share their knowledge with the class. If possible, share one or two of his poems so children get a feel for his style of writing.

Tell the children that in this lesson they will focus on one extract from Benjamin Zephaniah's autobiography. Then they will answer questions about the extract. Remind children that sometimes the answers to the questions will be clearly written in the extract, but that sometimes they may need to think a little harder and use their own ideas, supported by the text.

Ask the children to read the extract individually or in pairs. Ask them to note down any words they do not understand. Discuss unknown or unusual vocabulary before setting children to work answering the questions in the Pupil Book. Try to avoid discussing the content of the extract until after the children have answered the Pupil Book questions.

Unit 19: Non-fiction (autobiography): 'Benjamin Zephaniah: My Story'

Pupil practice

Pupil Book pages 77–78

Get started

Ask children to write sentences to answer the questions, using quotations where possible. **Suggested answers:**

1. Benjamin was 'born in Aston'. [1 mark]
2. Benjamin remembers Hockley to be 'very white – very poor, but very white'. [1 mark]
3. It was a busy household because Benjamin has 'seven brothers and sisters'. [1 mark]
4. Benjamin says he 'actually really liked a busy house, a house with lots of kids and lots of noise'. [1 mark]
5. There was only 'one comb in the house'. [1 mark]
6. When the children's shoes were worn out, 'instead of buying a new pair', Benjamin's dad would 'make new soles out of cardboard, so that they lasted longer'. [1 mark]
7. Benjamin asked his brother to watch him walk because he wanted to know if 'he could see the cardboard on my shoes'. [1 mark]
8. Benjamin stopped lifting his foot up behind him because he didn't want 'the other kids to see the cardboard'. [1 mark]

Try these

Ask children to write sentences to answer the questions, explaining their answers as fully as they can. The children's answers may be subjective but should be in their own words and well justified, using evidence from either the text or the children's own experiences. **Possible answers:**

1. Answers should state that, because they didn't have a bathroom inside the house in Hockley, Benjamin's family used 'an old tin bath in the communal back garden' to wash themselves. [1 mark]
2. Answers could suggest that Benjamin's parents were too busy to look after their eight children and were glad that Benjamin took care of them, that they thought Benjamin and his lessons were good for the children, or possibly that they didn't notice/care that Benjamin was controlling his siblings' behaviour. [1 mark]
3. Answers should detect that Benjamin was at least partly pleased when the school over the road closed down, as it meant he could take and use its exercise books. They could also suggest that Benjamin may also have been disappointed, as he obviously enjoyed learning or as he would now have to go to a school further away. [2 marks]
4. Answers should explain that Benjamin made his siblings play 'school' with him because he wanted to be the teacher and he was the boss. They could also add that he was keen to explore and share his knowledge and/or that he thought he could improve on their other lessons. [2 marks]
5. Answers should grasp that Benjamin and his siblings had to share a bed because the council house their family had wasn't big enough for, and/or that the family couldn't afford, separate beds. [2 marks]
6. Answers should detect that, although Benjamin comments that he avoided siblings with smelly feet (and could because he was 'the boss'), he otherwise doesn't complain about having to share a bed. He states earlier that he 'liked a busy house, a house with lots of kids and lots of noise', and seems therefore not to have minded very much about the cramped conditions. Answers may relate the situation to children's own contrasting experiences, but should attempt to convey Benjamin's opinions rather than their own. [2 marks]
7. Answers should appreciate that Benjamin's father mended their shoes 'instead of buying a new pair' in order to save money. [1 mark]
8. Answers should detect that, despite Benjamin's largely positive attitude towards his home life, he seems to have been concerned that the other children at school would detect his father's money-saving trick of resoling shoes with cardboard. They should conclude that Benjamin was, to some extent, embarrassed that his family was 'poor'. [2 marks]

Now try these

The children's answers will be subjective, but should be well justified where appropriate. **Possible answers:**

1. Answers could refer to Benjamin's positive attitude, love for his family, awareness of racial difference, practicality and resourcefulness in the face of financial hardship, domineering spirit, enthusiasm for education and concern about his family's reputation among his school friends. [3 marks max]
2. Open-ended question: Look for relevant questions directed at Benjamin that are not answered by the extract, for example: *Did you enjoy school? When did you realise you were good at poetry and writing? Did you have any other hobbies?* [3 marks max]
3. Open-ended question: Look for relevance to task, imagination, presentation and inclusion of details about Benjamin's childhood from the text (such as where he lived and his family members). [4 marks max]
4. Open-ended question: Answers should consider the main facts required to write an autobiography and follow on from the section 'A busy house'

Unit 19: Non-fiction (autobiography): 'Benjamin Zephaniah: My Story'

in the extract. They could mention schooling, hobbies, achievements, plans, feelings and any life-changing events. [3 marks max]

5. Open-ended question: Look for relevance to task, imagination, presentation and inclusion of details about Benjamin's childhood from the text. [3 marks max]

Support, embed & challenge

Support
Use Unit 19 Resource 1: Fact or opinion? to support children in understanding the personal and impersonal elements of an autobiography. Ask them to read through the text again and sort the information into two columns: 'Facts' or 'Opinions'.

Embed
Use Unit 19 Resource 2: Planning a lesson to encourage children to follow Benjamin's example and plan their own school lesson for younger siblings or friends. Help children to plan their main lesson points, if required. Then ask children to do some research around these points and prepare a presentation of their findings that can be shared with others.

Challenge
Ask children to research some poetry by Benjamin Zephaniah and find some more information about the poet himself. Ask them to be prepared to share their findings with the class or a group, and to prepare a reading of the poem(s) they find.

Homework / Additional activities

Poetry presentations
Ask children to prepare a presentation about a poem of their own (or about another piece of writing of which they are proud). Ask children to be prepared to share their presentation with the class or a group.

Unit 20: Non-fiction (information text): 'The Kingdom of Benin'

Overview

English curriculum objectives

- Continue to read and discuss an increasingly wide range of fiction, poetry, plays, non-fiction and reference books or textbooks
- Read books that are structured in different ways and read for a range of purposes
- Identify and discuss themes and conventions in and across a wide range of writing
- Check that the book makes sense to them, discussing their understanding and exploring the meaning of words in context
- Ask questions to improve their understanding
- Summarise the main ideas drawn from more than one paragraph, identifying key details that support the main idea
- Identify how language, structure and presentation contribute to meaning
- Distinguish between statements of fact and opinion
- Retrieve, record and present information from non-fiction
- Participate in discussions about books that are read to them and those they can read for themselves, building on their own and others' ideas and challenging views courteously
- Explain and discuss their understanding of what they have read, including through formal presentations and debates, maintaining a focus on the topic and using notes where necessary
- Provide reasoned justification for their views

Treasure House resources

- Comprehension Skills Pupil Book 6, Unit 20, pages 79–81
- Photocopiable Unit 20, Resource 1: Quick quiz, page 126
- Photocopiable Unit 20, Resource 2: Researching West Africa, page 127

Additional resources

- Dictionaries or the internet (optional)
- *The Kingdom of Benin* by Phillip Steele, whole text (optional)

Introduction

Teaching overview

The Kingdom of Benin is an information text. It presents factual information about how ancient civilisations developed in West Africa over thousands of years. Children are able to use the text to explore how language, structure and presentation contribute to meaning, as well as to discover more about the topic.

Introduce the extract

Ask the children if they have any prior knowledge of Africa and/or ancient civilisations. If they do, invite them to share their knowledge with the class.

Tell the children that in this lesson they will focus on an extract from an information text about civilisations that developed in Benin, in Africa. Then they will answer questions about the extract. Remind children that sometimes the answers to the questions will be clearly written in the extract, but that sometimes they may need to think a little harder and use their own ideas, supported by the text.

Ask the children to read the extract individually or in pairs. Ask them to note down any words they do not understand. Discuss unknown or unusual vocabulary before setting children to work answering the questions in the Pupil Book. Try to avoid discussing the content of the extract until after the children have answered the Pupil Book questions.

Unit 20: Non-fiction (information text): 'The Kingdom of Benin'

Pupil practice

Pupil Book pages 80–81

Get started

Ask children to write sentences to answer the questions, using quotations where possible. **Suggested answers:**

1. 'BCE' means 'before common era' and 'CE' means 'common era'. [2 marks]
2. The people of the Nok culture lived 'In the savannah zone, to the north of Benin'. [1 mark]
3. The iron working skills were eventually passed on to 'the peoples living in the rainforest, including the Edo'. [1 mark]
4. The extract says: 'Iron tools made it easier for them to clear parts of the forest.' [1 mark]
5. They cleared parts of the forest 'to plant crops and build villages'. [1 mark]
6. The 'origins of the rainforest peoples' and 'their history' became mixed up with myths and legends. [1 mark]
7. The first powerful kingdom in the area was set up by 'the Yoruba people to the northwest of Benin'. [1 mark]
8. The Edo founded their kingdom 'by the 900s CE'. [1 mark]

Try these

Ask children to write sentences to answer the questions, explaining their answers as fully as they can. The children's answers may be subjective but should be in their own words and well justified, using evidence from either the text or the children's own experiences. **Possible answers:**

1. Answers could suggest that the Nok culture passed on their iron working skills to the peoples living in the rainforest simply through altruism or because they would benefit if these people could 'clear parts of the forest'. They could also make the connection that this may have been as a form of trade, or because the peoples may have joined together to 'defend their lands from attack'. [2 marks]
2. Answers could assert that it was important that the history of the rainforest peoples was passed on because it mattered to them as a clan and/or because it taught them something, or that it was not important as progress continued despite much of the history being 'mixed up with myths and legends'. [1 mark]
3. Answers should identify that the Edo people had close connections with 'the Yoruba who lived in the area to the north west of Benin', and that they are likely to have shared several ways of life due to their physical proximity. They may add that the people may have interacted through trade, or because they may have joined together to 'defend their lands from attack'. [2 marks]
4. Answers should identify that a 'clan' is a group of people 'descended from the same ancestor', and so that we more commonly call clans 'families' in English. [1 mark]
5. Answers should identify that some clans joined together 'in order to trade more effectively or defend their lands from attack', and that some 'settlements joined together under a king' or chief. [2 marks]
6. Answers are likely to suggest that different age groups are best suited to different duties because of their different abilities (for example, because younger people are stronger and/or faster, and older people have more experience). [2 marks]
7. Answers should acknowledge that Ife was the first powerful kingdom in the Edo region, and also offer at least one reason it may have been influential. They could suggest that it created laws or traditions that affected the other peoples in the region, or created different ways of trading and/or fighting. [2 marks]
8. Answers could suggest that small, individual clans were less able to defend themselves, had poorer trade links and/or otherwise offered less to the people who remained within them than larger settlements did. [2 marks]

Now try these

The children's answers will be subjective, but should be well justified where appropriate. **Possible answers:**

1. Open-ended question: Look for accurate definitions of the key or more difficult words in the extract (for example 'civilisations', 'clans', 'descended', 'ancestors', 'advisors'). The words should be presented alphabetically. [3 marks max]
2. Answers could include the following dates and events as mentioned in the text:
   - 550 BCE: people of the Nok culture learn to work and shape iron
   - 600s CE: Yoruba people set up the first powerful kingdom
   - 900s CE: Edo found their own kingdom

   Answers may also include other information from the text, if children deduce that it has been written in chronological order. [3 marks max]
3. Answers could mention that the sub-headings break up the text and make it easier to read, help the reader to find specific pieces of information quickly and/or signpost the topic of the following paragraph(s). [2 marks]

Unit 20: Non-fiction (information text): 'The Kingdom of Benin'

4. Answers should mention that the maps help the reader to understand the geographical locations of the places and peoples mentioned in the text (and other nearby places), the nature of the environment in West Africa and how Benin grew from the 1400s to the 1600s. [3 marks max]

5. Open-ended question: Look for relevance to task, accuracy of details given in the extract, imagination and presentation. [3 marks max]

Support, embed & challenge

Support
Use Unit 20 Resource 1: Quick quiz to support children in grounding the knowledge they have gained from the extract as they create a short quiz on it. Ask children to come up with ten questions that the extract can answer, and swap their quizzes with their partners.

Embed
Use Unit 20 Resource 2: Researching West Africa to encourage children to conduct further research about West Africa. Help children to plan their questions, if required. For example, ask: 'Where is Africa?', 'How big is it?', 'What wildlife is there in West Africa?', 'What are people's homes like nowadays?' Then ask children to research the answers to their questions and present their findings as either a fact file or a presentation that can be shared with others.

Challenge
Ask children to research more about the kingdom of Benin, starting from the point when the extract ends. Ask them to refer to the structure and style of the extract to help them to write their reports.

Homework / Additional activities

What happens next?
Ask children to research and create a short presentation about another ancient civilisation: ancient Greece, ancient Rome, ancient Britain or ancient Egypt. Ask them to come prepared to share their presentation with the class or a group.

Review unit 3: Poetry: 'Sullen Jane' and 'Competition'

Pupil Book pages 82–85

Get started

Ask children to write sentences to answer the questions, using quotations where possible.

Suggested answers:

1. Jane's 'mouth turns down all tight and hard / Like a trap that's just snapped shut.' Answers could also mention that Jane 'grinds her teeth' and that her 'jaw begins to jut'. [2 marks]

2. If you smile to cheer Jane up, she 'just wrinkles up her nose / And heaves a mournful sigh'. [1 mark]

3. The speaker's (and Jane's) grandmother fixes Jane's sulky dumps. [1 mark]

4. The speaker says that Jane's moans are put into 'a tin' and emptied into 'the garden rubbish bin'. [1 mark]

5. To look sadder than you, the speaker can 'cry like a tap / At the drop of a hat'. [1 mark]

6. To make himself/herself fatter than you, the speaker can 'eat fourteen tons / Of gigantic iced buns'. [1 mark]

7. When the speaker shouts his/her name, 'windows shatter in Spain'. [1 mark]

8. Both poems are about negative behaviour or badly behaved children. 'Sullen Jane' is about moodiness and 'Competition' is about boasting. [1 mark]

Try these

Ask children to write sentences to answer the questions, explaining their answers as fully as they can. The children's answers may be subjective but should be in their own words and well justified, using evidence from either the text or the children's own experiences.

Possible answers:

1. Answers should conclude that the speaker is Sullen Jane's cousin. In the poem Jane is introduced as 'sullen cousin Jane'. [1 mark]

2. Open-ended question: Answers could refer to the characters' family bond, but should also acknowledge less straightforward indications: the speaker's initial concern ('Oh what can be the matter / With sullen cousin Jane?'), repeated efforts to cheer Jane up ('No matter how you try'), informal manner ('Jane, what's up?') and/or caution ('you simply daren't go near her, you daren't say a thing'). [2 marks]

3. Answers should recognise that using words such as 'sulky dumplings' and 'grumpified' to describe Jane's mood adds humour to and lightens the tone of the poem. They could also comment that these descriptions refuse to take Jane's moods seriously. [2 marks]

4. Answers should infer that what makes Jane feel better is being able to talk about her problems, and/or imagine them being discarded, and/or learning to take them less seriously. [2 marks]

5. Answers should identify the similes as 'Her mouth turns down all tight and hard / Like a trap that's just snapped shut' and 'Her face is like a frozen lake / That the kindest word can't crack'. They should comment that the effect of both similes is to create an image in the reader's mind of how Jane's sullen face looks. They could add that the comparisons also suggest that her expression shares other attributes with the trap and the frozen lake, for example that it causes pain and feels cold. [2 marks]

6. Open-ended question: Answers could speculate that the speaker wants attention and/or feels insecure, or is simply very competitive – although it is unlikely that the speaker genuinely wants to prove his/her superiority at being sad, lying or getting fat. Answers may also probe a little further and suggest that the speaker is trying to stop the listener from being sad, lying, feeling fat and shouting. [2 marks max]

7. Answers should recognise that the first and third lines of each verse in 'Sullen Jane' rhyme (ABCB). In 'Competition', lines three and four of each verse form a rhyming couplet, and lines two and five end in the same word (ABCCB). [2 marks]

8. Answers should recognise that both poems end in a positive manner. 'Sullen Jane' ends by describing Jane's 'bright and shining grin', and 'Competition' ends with humour, when the speaker is interrupted with the comment, 'Pardon?' [2 marks]

Review unit 3: Poetry: 'Sullen Jane' and 'Competition'

Now try these

The children's answers will be subjective, but should be well justified where appropriate.

Possible answers:

1. Answers should suggest that the poet wrote the poems to make humorous observations about bad behaviour. Suggestions for his intended audience could include (but aren't limited to) people who have to deal with bad behaviour (to entertain them, as they will recognise what he observes), or children at risk of behaving in this way (to help them see how their behaviour looks to others). [3 marks max]

2. Answers could note that each poem has a strong beat but irregular rhythm. 'Sullen Jane' contains two strong beats in each line, and varying numbers of syllables. 'Competition' also varies the number of syllables in its lines, but contains three strong beats in lines one, two and five of each verse, and two strong beats in lines three and four. This gives both poems a lyrical tone, making them easy to read and adding to their light-hearted, positive and humorous nature. [3 marks max]

3. Answers could suggest that the repetition of the structure of the verses in 'Competition' adds further to the humour and lyrical nature of the poem, and also builds a clear image of a competitive and confrontational speaker. [3 marks max]

4. Answers should recognise that the change in pattern of the final verse in 'Competition' makes the poem end abruptly, as if the speaker is being interrupted. They could add that this draws attention to the speaker's silliness and/or adds an amusing punchline to the poem. [3 marks max]

5. Open-ended question: Look for relevance to task, consistency of characters and theme, imagination and presentation. [3 marks max]

Unit 1 Resource 1

Amy's character

Use the text and your own ideas to create a character profile of Amy.

Picture	Name
	Age

Family details

Physical description	Personality

Likes	Dislikes

Unit 1 Resource 2

Richard's view

Imagine that Richard is chatting to his sister. Retell the events in the extract from Richard's point of view.

Unit 2 Resource 1

The little big comic strip

Retell the story as a comic strip. Look carefully at the number of panels in the template and where the thought and speech bubbles are placed.

Unit 2 Resource 2

Morals

Research and discuss the morals below. Try to explain them in your own words.

Being smart is more important than being strong.

No matter how small you are, you can still help others.

Be careful with your words.

Don't judge others on appearances.

Treat others as you would like to be treated.

Unit 3 Resource 1

Bike advert

Highlight and discuss the persuasive features on this advert.

New Stanley Pro 3000

- Endorsed by world-champion mountain-bike racer, Dan Doonan
- Reinforced titanium frame and bespoke braking system
- Crafted using over 30 years' experience
- Award-winning concept
- Available in all good cycle stores

Special offer launch price: only £345 – a massive saving of over £100!

Get it now! Be the envy of your whole street!

Unit 3 Resource 2

Bike questionnaire

Imagine you have been given the task of designing an advert for the new Stanley Pro 3000 bike. Carry out research to find out what would persuade people in your class to buy it.

Plan questions to ask:

Record your findings here:

Unit 4 Resource 1

For and against

Find the arguments for and against proving climate change in the text and add them to the correct column. Then research further arguments to add to the table.

Arguments to prove climate change	Arguments to disprove climate change

Unit 4 Resource 2

An email to Pete

Write an email to Pete, explaining your own opinion on climate change. Use what you have read in the emails and your own research.

New Message

To

Subject

Send

Unit 5 Resource 1

Countdown summary

In your own words, summarise the point Darren's mum makes after each number in the countdown. One example is given.

Ten	The weather outside is horrible.
Nine	
Eight	
Seven	
Six	
Five	
Four	
Three	
Two	
One	
'Half a second, a quarter, an eighth'	

Unit 5 Resource 2

My countdown poem

Use this grid to plan your own poem counting down to an event.

The event: _____

Ten	
Nine	
Eight	
Seven	
Six	
Five	
Four	
Three	
Two	
One	

Unit 6 Resource 1

Finding the beat

Look at the rhythm of the first verse. In the first two lines, the syllables that form the poem's beat are underlined.

Count the syllables in the other lines and underline the beats.

<u>By</u> the <u>shin</u>ing <u>Big</u>-Sea-<u>Wa</u>ter,

<u>Stood</u> the <u>wig</u>wam <u>of</u> No<u>ko</u>mis,

Daughter of the Moon, Nokomis.

Dark behind it rose the forest,

Rose the black and gloomy pine-trees,

Rose the first with cones upon them;

Bright before it beat the water,

Beat the clear and sunny water,

Beat the shining Big-Sea-Water.

From 'The Song of Hiawatha' by H. W. Longfellow

Unit 6 Resource 2

Hiawatha's brothers

Research and make notes about the characteristics of these animals from 'The Song of Hiawatha'. You could then use your notes to add more information to the final verse of the extract.

Reindeer

Bears

Owlets

Beavers

Squirrels

Rabbits

Unit 7 Resource 1

Three diaries

Describe the events in the extract from each character's point of view. Write a short paragraph for each diary.

The highwayman's diary:

Bess's diary:

Tim's diary:

Unit 7 Resource 2

The highwayman's character

Use the text and your own ideas to create a character profile of the highwayman.

Picture	Name
	Age

Relationships

Physical description	Personality

Likes	Dislikes

Unit 8 Resource 1

Latest news

Here is the news story without any of the extra report features.

Latest news | Indepth news | Traffic news

Water levels at an all-time low

The water companies have been given just three weeks to come up with plans to explain how they will respond to the current water shortage and to the long-term need to provide water for homes while, at the same time, protecting our rivers.

Leakage is the top priority. At present an average of 30% of treated water leaks away before it can be used.

Among the plans to be considered is for the water companies to offer to repair leaks on customers' land free of charge.

Another way of saving water is for every home to use water more carefully.

A way of encouraging this would be to introduce water meters in every household. "If people knew they had to pay for every drop of water they use," said one water company spokesman yesterday, "they would soon be far more conservation minded!"

But the government is reserving its position on water meters. Apart from the extra cost of installing meters, they wonder about the fairness for people with large families, or those with medical conditions requiring frequent bathing, or whose work makes them dirty.

Unit 8 Resource 2

Alternative solutions

Consider these more extreme solutions to water shortages.

Re-using sewage water

- Waste water can be purified, and is completely clean and safe to drink.
- Some countries already use this method successfully.
- It costs money to purify the water.
- People in the UK have a negative perception of drinking this water.

Building new reservoirs

- Water companies would like to invest in storing more water ready for the shortages.
- Building new reservoirs would cost billions of pounds.
- They can take a long time to build.

Fitting cross-country pipelines

- The north of the country has more rainfall, so a pipeline could be fitted to transport it to the south.
- This would be very expensive.

Using sea water

- As we live on an island, there is plenty of sea water all around us.
- Seawater can be desalinated, which means the salt can be taken out and it can be made pure enough for drinking.
- This is an expensive process.
- There is no plan regarding what to do with the leftover salt.
- Some environmentalists say this could harm marine life.

Unit 9 Resource 1

Desert animals

Read the passages below. Then create three questions about each passage. Ask a partner to answer them.

The roadrunner

The roadrunner is a desert bird that rarely flies. Instead, it prefers to run at speeds of up to 18 miles per hour. It averages about 20 inches in length and 19 inches in wingspan. Despite spending most of its time running along the ground, the roadrunner likes to nest in trees and shrubs.

One way it is suited to desert life is that it does not need to drink water to survive! This is so long as it can eat prey that has a high water content, such as insects, small birds, lizards, snakes and fruit.

Questions about this passage:

1. _____

2. _____

3. _____

The kangaroo rat

This animal looks like a rat – but, when it gets excited, it can jump up to two feet high and as far as six feet along!

The kangaroo rat is suited to desert life because it is nocturnal. During the day, it stays in its underground burrow, with the entrance blocked with sand to keep predators out. It comes out at night to hunt for food such as seeds, insects and flowers.

The kangaroo rat manages to get most of the water it needs from the seeds it eats and stores in its burrow.

Questions about this passage:

1. _____

2. _____

3. _____

Unit 9 Resource 2

Continuing 'Deserts'

Read the passage below and give it a title.

| Title: |

Despite their harsh conditions, deserts are home to many living things. Plants and animals have had to adapt to survive in the dry climate. Many animals that live in deserts are nocturnal, sleeping during the day when it is hottest and coming out in the cooler night to eat and hunt.

Now think up ideas for four more subheadings that could introduce further information you could include if you were continuing the text about deserts.

- _____
- _____
- _____
- _____

Now choose one of your subheadings and research information to write its section. Make notes here:

Unit 10 Resource 1

Painting a picture

Similes and metaphors are figures of speech. They help a writer paint a clear picture for a reader.

Similes compare one thing to another, usually using the words 'like' or 'as'.

For example: 'My independence melts away / Like a snowman in the sun.'

What two things are being compared in these lines?

The girl's _____ is being compared to a _____.

Metaphors suggest that one thing is or becomes another.

For example: 'Winter is the king of showmen'

In this line, what two things is the writer suggesting are the same?

The writer suggests that _____ really is a _____.

Now read the sentences below. At the end of each sentence, write either 'simile' or 'metaphor' to show which figure of speech appears in the sentence.

1. Peter was as cool as a cucumber when he threw the snowball.

2. The snow was a glittery blanket.

3. The garden was as pretty as a picture.

4. My toes were icicles.

Unit 10 Resource 2

Similes and metaphors

Read the sentences below. At the end of each sentence, write either 'simile' or 'metaphor' to show which figure of speech appears in the sentence.

1. Peter was as cool as a cucumber when he threw the snowball.

2. The snow was a glittery blanket.

3. The garden was as pretty as a picture.

4. My toes were icicles.

5. Amy ran through the snow – she was a runaway train, off the tracks.

6. The spy was as slippery as an eel.

Use words from the word box below (or choose your own words) to write three similes and three metaphors of your own. You may use each word more than once.

| sun | lion | fire | glowing | fast | fierce | brave | golden | blazing |
| snowflakes | glittery | disco ball | sugar | gentle | girl | boy |

Similes:

1. _____

2. _____

3. _____

Metaphors:

1. _____

2. _____

3. _____

Unit 11 Resource 1

About the boy

Use the text and your own ideas to create a character profile of the boy Milo meets in the forest.

Picture	Name
	Age

Family details

Physical description	Personality

Details about where he lives

Unit 11 Resource 2

Idioms

Idioms are a form of figurative language. An idiom is a phrase or group of words that has a figurative meaning that differs from its literal meaning.

Look at this list of idioms. What do they mean? Discuss, research and write a definition for each one.

1. That test was a piece of cake.
2. She really let the cat out of the bag.
3. Break a leg in the play!
4. I was being kept in the dark.
5. My uncle tries to pull everyone's leg.
6. I've been burning the candle at both ends.
7. She's been pulling the wool over your eyes.
8. He's been leading you up the garden path.
9. You're driving me round the bend.
10. I'm all ears.
11. She wouldn't hurt a fly.
12. It's raining cats and dogs.
13. My mum treats me with kid gloves.
14. He was like a bull in a china shop.
15. He was like a kid in a sweet shop.
16. It's an inside joke.
17. My dad hit the roof.
18. I'll catch you later.
19. I have a bone to pick with you.
20. She's turned over a new leaf.

Unit 12 Resource 1

Ruth's diary

Read the extract again, noticing what Ruth knows, sees and thinks. Fill in Ruth's diary, using this information from the text and your own ideas.

Today, I saw …

The mistress looked like …

At first, I thought …

Now, I think …

Unit 12 Resource 2

Hiding the truth

Imagine you are Mother. You have just been told some terrible news. How do you feel and what do you decide to do?

What bad news have you been told?

What are your true feelings about it?

Will you tell the children everything?

What precisely will you say to the children?

Unit 13 Resource 1

Gulliver's comic strip

Retell the story as a comic strip. Look carefully at the number of panels in the template and where the thought and speech bubbles are placed.

Unit 13 Resource 2

A strange language

The author of 'Gulliver's Travels' had to invent a new language for Lilliput. Can you invent a language of your own?

First think of new words for the English words below and then add your own.

Words in English	Words in your new language
the	
a	
you	
I	
girl	
boy	
book	
table	
trees	
is / are / am	
sit / sits	
run / runs	
play / plays	
near	
on	
to	
under	

Now try creating sentences with your new words.

Can you use them to write a message your partner could understand?

Unit 14 Resource 1

Finding the features

Label the start of the playscript with the features below.

The character speaking	Stage directions	Character speech	List of characters	Scene heading

CHARACTERS
　A King
　Compere Lapin
　Compere Tig
　The King's guards
　A wise man

SCENE 1

(King enters downstage left. A wise man follows closely behind him.)

KING: Ah, look at my beautiful pool. It is so lovely and fresh. I cannot wait to bathe in it.

(The King bends down to look in the water. The water changes from a clear blue to a murky colour.)

KING: (Furiously) Who has been bathing in my pool? The water is murky and dirty!

Unit 14 Resource 2

A new trick

Plan a new story for the trickster character of Compere Lapin. First, think up a good trick he could try!

What trick will Compere Lapin decide to play?

Whom does he want to trick?

How will this character turn the trick back on Compere Lapin?

What will happen to Compere Lapin in the end?

Unit 15 Resource 1

Questions about China

Read the passages below. Then create three questions about each passage. Ask a partner to answer them.

People in China

China is the world's most populated country. There are over 1.35 billion people in China. That's more than twice the number of people in Europe, and one billion more than in the United States!

Chinese is the most widely spoken language in the world. There are thousands of different forms of the Chinese language, called dialects. The dialect that is taught in schools and used for national radio and TV broadcasts is Mandarin Chinese, which is China's official language.

Questions about this passage:

1. _____

2. _____

3. _____

Animals in China

Wildlife in China is very diverse. There are over 30 000 kinds of plants and over 4400 species of vertebrates! Because of the huge area China covers, there is a great range of different climates and landscapes to support life.

This means China is home to many amazing animals, including tigers, alligators, camels and giant pandas.

Sadly, the fast growth of cities and towns in China means that the natural environments of many of these animals has been destroyed. Many of them are currently listed as endangered species.

Questions about this passage:

1. _____

2. _____

3. _____

Unit 15 Resource 2

Researching China

Use this sheet to help you to research more about China.

Plan six questions about China you would like to answer:

1. _____
2. _____
3. _____
4. _____
5. _____
6. _____

Now do research to find the answers to your questions. Make notes here:

How will you present your information? Plan it here:

Unit 16 Resource 1

Poem pieces

Fill in the gaps to begin your own poem about a different bad habit. If you'd like to make lines rhyme, feel free to change some other words, too.

A trick that everyone abhors

Is _____.

A _____'s little _____

Who lived in _____

(By name _____),

Was given to this furious sport.

They would deliberately go

And _____!

Now try to continue the poem, using the text of 'Rebecca' for guidance.

Unit 16 Resource 2

Poem planner

Use this planning sheet to structure your ideas for a poem of your own.

Then write your poem. How funny will you make it?

The bad habit

The culprit

The habit's effects

The dreadful end

Unit 17 Resource 1

Briony's character

Use the text and your own ideas to create a character profile of Briony, the speaker in the extract.

Picture	Name
	Age

Family details

Physical description	Personality

Likes	Dislikes

© HarperCollins*Publishers* 2017

Unit 17 Resource 2

Bright Spark storyboard

Imagine you are directing a television adaptation of the extract. Plan how each shot will look. What camera positions will there be? What things will you show and when? Then write a voiceover of Briony's thoughts so the viewer can hear them.

1.	2.	3.

Voiceover:

4.	5.	6.

Voiceover:

7.	8.	9.

Voiceover:

© HarperCollins*Publishers* 2017

Unit 18 Resource 1

Making decisions

Find each decision the man makes during the events in the extract.

Then use either the text or your imagination to give a reason for it. The decisions don't have to be listed in order.

One example is given.

Decision	Reason
• The man got off the rickety train.	• Everyone in his carriage was asleep.

Unit 18 Resource 2

Timeline

Create a timeline of everything you know has happened to the speaker in the extract, using both the text and your imagination. Start with his first encounter with Scudder (the dead man), and end with him waking up in the heather to catch the train.

Unit 19 Resource 1

Fact or opinion?

Read the extract again and sort each piece of information into one of these two columns.

Facts	Opinions and feelings

Unit 19 Resource 2

Planning a lesson

Use this sheet to help you to follow **Benjamin's** example and plan a lesson of your own!

Plan three lesson points you would like to cover:

1. _____

2. _____

3. _____

Now research your lesson points to make sure you can explain them.

Make notes here:

How will you present your lesson? Plan it here:

Unit 20 Resource 1

Quick quiz

Test your partner's knowledge about the Kingdom of Benin! Come up with ten questions that can be answered from the extract. Then swap your quiz with a partner.

Questions	Answers
1.	
2.	
3.	
4.	
5.	
6.	
7.	
8.	
9.	
10.	

Unit 20 Resource 2

Researching West Africa

Use this sheet to help you to research more about West Africa. Plan six questions about West Africa you would like to answer:

1. _____
2. _____
3. _____
4. _____
5. _____
6. _____

Now do research to find the answers to your questions. Make notes here:

How will you present your information? Plan it here: